Landscape to Light

Landscape to Light

Neil M. Gunn

compiled by
Alistair McCleery and Dairmid Gunn

Whittles Publishing

Published by
Whittles Publishing Ltd.,
Dunbeath,
Caithness, KW6 6EY,
Scotland, UK
www.whittlespublishing.com

ISBN 978-1904445-90-6

Printed and Bound by Digital Book Print
Unit 10, Avant Business Centre, Denbigh West
Milton Keynes, MK1 1DR
Tel:01908 377084
Email: enquiries@digitalbookprint.com

Contents

Contents

Introduction

NEIL M GUNN (1891 – 1973), one of Scotland's most distinguished and highly regarded novelists of the 20th century, was a prolific writer. While he is best known for his fictional work Gunn was also a perceptive and meditative essayist and he wrote extensively throughout his life on a wide range of subjects from landscape, nature and fishing to politics, nationalism and current affairs. This collection of essays concentrates on his writings on his native landscape and culture and the spiritual aspects of life and thought. These essays, written in parallel with his novels, mirror most clearly many of the ideas and speculations that inform the novels. Like the novels, the essays provide a chart of the author's literary and spiritual journey through life. The essays selected for *Landscape to Light* are an invitation to join the author on this journey; their cumulative effect can lead not only to a greater understanding of the novelist himself but also to a more enlightening and imaginative way of looking at events, both past and present. In addition to being complementary to the novels, the selected essays cover the period beyond Gunn's last major work, *The Atom of Delight* (1956) and dwell on the questions and observations made in that remarkable work.

Neil Gunn, the son of a successful fishing boat skipper, was born in the small coastal village of Dunbeath in Scotland's most northerly county, Caithness, in which fishing and crofting were the principal means of livelihood. After an idyllic childhood in a landscape of moor, river and sea, Gunn was sent to pursue his secondary education at the hands of a tutor engaged by an elder sister married to a doctor in the south-western county of Kirkcudbrightshire. From this tutor he received a sound grounding in English literature and a sufficient grasp of mathematics to pass the entrance examination for the Civil Service in 1907. Four years later he began his career in the Customs and Excise Service, which was to take him back to the Highlands where during the First World War he combined his customs and excise duties as a substitute officer with War work for the Admiralty. It was during these years that he developed a life-long friendship with the Irish novelist to be, Maurice Walsh, who was also a customs and excise officer. In 1921 he married a Highland girl from Dingwall, the county town of Ross and Cromarty, and two years later returned to the North. He was shocked to find Caithness in serious economic and social decline; fishing and crofting were particularly affected by the national economic crisis and evidence of this was to be seen in badly surfaced roads, inadequate fencing and silted-up harbours. All this acted as stimulus for Gunn to indulge his creative instincts by writing. He had already written many articles and short stories, but not a novel. That was to come in 1926 when he was comfortably settled in Inverness on duties connected with the local Glen Mohr distillery. *The Grey Coast* (1926) and its successor, *The Lost Glen* (1932) were books in the realist mode, which reflected Gunn's bitterness and pessimism at that time. Neither book enjoyed much success. That had to await the appearance of a book written after *The Lost Glen,* but published before it, *Morning Tide* (1931). A Book Society choice, *Morning Tide* nurtured Gunn's belief that the past had much to offer in terms of being the source of guidance in his search for a vision of renewal and regeneration. Describing the strength and diversity of rural community life in the village of his childhood, the book exudes a freshness and vigour that can only delight. Within the ingredients provided by the vicissitudes experienced by a community living with the dangers of making a living from the sea and the constant sadness of increasing emigration, the book contains a kernel of hope for the future in the life of the boy so central to the freshness and life of the story. Although urged by an enthusiastic publisher for more of the same, Gunn instead chose to explore in his next two books different territory, but this time in the distant past. *Sun Circle* (1933) is a highly imaginative account of the genesis of Caithness during the Viking incursions of the 8th and 9th centuries with the clash of races, Celtic, Pictish and Norse and the interaction of their ways of life and beliefs. *Sun Circle* was followed by *Butcher's Broom* (1934), a fictitious account of the Clearances in the late 18th and early 19th centuries when rural communities were evicted from their lands to make way for sheep farming. This emotive subject is handled sensitively and movingly by Gunn in a way that brings out the acute sense of betrayal of a people by their hereditary chiefs and signals the end of an important part of the Celtic community structure. The two books were to form part of a natural trilogy that was rounded off by the addition of a later book *The Silver Darlings* (1941) set in the herring boom in the early 19th century – a trilogy that charts the fortunes of a people from a stormy and unsettled birth through periods of quiet settlement and brutal dispossession to the success of the their encounter with the sea, and freedom.

The book that changed the course of Gunn's life and literary career was written in 1937 under the title of *Highland River*. The river is the river of his childhood and concerns at one level the exploration of it from estuary to source. The river is also an analogue for a life, and Gunn's quest is to find the source of meaning within himself. Reflected in the story, which is written in biographical form, are Gunn's own childhood experiences of the river and his later journey along its banks and those of his immediate younger brother, John, who fought in the First World War and read science at university at the time of the great advances in nuclear physics. The combined and wide range of experiences gives the book an extra dimension and makes it relevant to the confused and rudderless world of the 1930s. The book, highly acclaimed, was awarded the prestigious James Tait Black Memorial prize, and on the strength of this Gunn decided to become a full-time writer. In an act of bravado Gunn, having resigned from the Customs and Excise Service, sold his house in Inverness and bought a 30-foot motor boat, in which he completed a voyage round the Inner Hebrides. He recorded his adventures and musings in *Off in a Boat* (1938) – a book that captivates both the practical seaman and the reflective voyager alike. It was a dramatic start to Gunn's career as a full-time writer.

With the adventure over, Gunn had to begin the serious search for a house that offered him the peaceful and tranquil atmosphere necessary for creative work. The house eventually chosen was Braefarm House situated in the hills to the north of Dingwall, his wife's home town; there he was to write eleven novels and a series of essays on country life that were restorative reading for the War years and their immediate aftermath. He started by exploring some of the ideas emanating from his earlier novels in settings and milieu totally different from those of his childhood; in *Wild Geese Overhead* (1939) he chose the city of Glasgow and in *Second Sight* (1940) a deer forest and shooting lodge. In both he explored the inevitable clash between extreme rationalism and an intuitive and instinctive approach to living.

For the next eleven years Gunn was in his writing prime; he wrote prolifically and thoughtfully. He was happily settled in a comfortable house which enjoyed a broad open outlook; he had access to woodland, hill and moor for the afternoon walks that meant so much to him. Ever the craftsman, he used his observations of the countryside and the thoughts they engendered to colour his essays. These, in turn, informed his fictional work, and some of them are contained in this collection.

Wild Geese Overhead and *Second Sight* were written during the research and gestation period for Gunn's greatest novel *The Silver Darlings* (1941), a book that completed the trilogy of *Sun Circle* and *Butcher's Broom*; it is, however, much more than a magnificent epic of the herring boom of the late 18th and early 19th centuries; it shows the regeneration of a community displaced by the Clearances and contains within its awe-inspiring descriptions of men making a living in the inhospitable and threatening ambience of storms and treacherous seas the simple and moving story of the intricate and moving relationships between a mother, son and lover. Throughout this enthralling story there is a subtle interweaving of action and metaphysical speculation and a constant feeling of optimism and hope.

Nothing could be more different in physical scope than the book that followed *The Silver Darlings* with its title of *Young Art and Old Hector* (1942). It takes the form of an enchanting dialogue between a young boy and an old man – the present talking to the past. Gunn was to use the pair again as the main protagonists in his Orwellian novel, *The Green Isle of the Great Deep* (1944) – a novel that predates Orwell's famous '1984' by several years. It uses a rural setting rather than an urban one for the struggle by Art and Hector to preserve their individuality and freedom of thought in the totalitarian state in which they find themselves. They emerged from their ordeal unscathed because of their attachment to a way of life that had evolved from the distant past and was still in evidence in their home village. The book was particularly apposite for the 1940s when the totalitarian regimes of Nazi Germany and Soviet Russia were part of the world scene. Between the writing of the two books Gunn had clarified much of his thinking at that time in the novel *The Serpent* (1943). It is the story of an intellectual rebel who returns to his homeland after having lived in the city for a large part of his life and who muses philosophically on all his varied experiences. The setting for this book is the countryside around Braefarm House.

Gunn was to write five more novels and complete a series of essays before he had to leave the Heights of Brae because of the expiry of a rental agreement in 1949. The novels have a variety of themes – murder in a close and remote community and its implications for personal relationships in *The Key of the Chest* (1945) – the return of a failed student to his native community and his rehabilitation and eventual success in *The Drinking Well* (1946) – the escape to spiritual and mental health in the Highlands by a young woman from a blitzed London and Marxist circle there in *The Shadow* (1948) – an archaeological quest that led to the discovery and loss of a crock of gold and the finding of a metaphorical treasure that made life worth living in *The Silver Bough* (1948) – and the escape through an enriching and fortifying cultural background from a world on the brink of nuclear conflict during the Cold War in *The Lost Chart* (1949). Running through all the novels is a thread of speculative thought on a variety of matters such as human relationships, the individual's duty to his community, the aridity of social engineering and the place of the past in human activity as a source of guidance and wisdom.

The expiry of the rental agreement in 1949 marked another turning point for Neil Gunn in his literary and everyday life. The tenor of that life is beautifully reflected in a collection of essays of the Braefarm House years that was published in book form under the title of *Highland Pack* (1949). The enforced exodus from the landscape he loved and the cessation of a pattern of living that suited him heralded a change of focus for much of his later work. He began a deeper exploration of what he called 'the inner landscape' through selective reading and revelatory experiences in his own life to illuminate his search for self-realisation and ultimate meaning.

His next move was to a house (Kincraig) situated off the road between Dingwall and Evanton on the western side of the Cromarty Firth. It commanded extensive views of the Firth and the Black Isle, but it was overlooked and close to the main road to the North. It was not the haven Gunn had imagined as the necessary peace and quiet were lacking. Nevertheless, whilst there he managed to complete a collection of short stories, *The White Hour* (1950), some of which were improved versions of those from an earlier collection, *Hidden Doors* (1929), and a picaresque novel that was both innovative and explorative, *The Well at the World's End* (1951). This novel is a clear exposition of the development of Gunn's thinking at that time and is best described when he himself writes about it. 'Where most novels of the more ambitious kind today deal with violence and materialism leading to negation or despair, I thought it might be a change if I got a character who would wander among his fellows looking for the positive aspects of life. Is it possible to pierce the negative husk, the dark cloud, even for few moments, and come on the light, the bubbling well at the end of the fairy tale?'

In 1951 he moved from Kincraig to the village of Cannich in Strath Glass in Inverness-shire. A stretch of fishing on the right bank of the River Glass went with the large house Gunn had chosen (Kerrow). There he was to write his final three books – all very different from each other. On the surface *Blood Hunt* (1952) is a simple, beautifully balanced story of murder and revenge in a remote and peaceful community. Its fascination lies in a good man's positive and loving response to the events in his effort to preserve the wholeness of the community and eradicate the consequences of the negative and evil intrusion into its life. The second book, *The Other Landscape* (1954) could be called Gunn's *Tempest*; it tackles the impossible, and in it Gunn's metaphysical and aesthetic speculation reaches new heights. The use of the first person by an articulate and interested observer in the novel draws the speculation closer to the reader, and in stronger form. This disturbing novel brings into focus the long distance covered by Gunn in his spiritual pilgrimage through life – from the grim realism of *The Grey Coast* to an intensive search for meaning, self realisation and light in a seemingly uncaring world In *The Other Landscape*.

But the pilgrimage had not ended; in 1956 Gunn wrote his so-called spiritual autobiography, *The Atom of Delight*. This bears no resemblance to the accepted form of autobiography as a series of facts and dates in chronological order; it is simply a random description of experiences and books that have had an influence on Gunn's life. These included an encounter with Zen Buddhism in a book called *Zen in the Art of Archery* gifted to him in 1953 by a great friend who appreciated his interests and the direction of his thinking and who was to become one of his biographers. Zen was to play an important part in Gunn's thought processes in the years that followed. In Zen Gunn discovered something he already knew. In the philosophies of Zen Buddhism and Taoism Gunn recognised the moments of perception and insight as aspects he had known an experienced throughout his highland life. After *The Atom of Delight* it was goodbye to books, but not to essays. Those of a philosophical nature and with frequent allusions to Far Eastern philosophy were to become a continuation of some of the themes explored in the autobiography.

In 1960 Gunn made his final move to a spacious and comfortable house in its own grounds (Dalcraig) near the village of North Kessock on the Black Isle. It was a well-chosen haven with a fine view of the Beauly Firth and access to a quiet road by the shore. He was only there for three years when he suffered the irreparable loss of his wife 'Daisy' who had provided the richly warm atmosphere in all the houses in which they had lived together; she was the gardener too, and this Gunn greatly appreciated. After her death he continued to write articles and essays, some of which are included in this collection. A year before his death in 1973 he was informed by the Scottish Arts Council of the creation of a Neil Gunn International Fellowship for authors of distinction in the English speaking world as a token of the high regard and esteem in which he was held in literary circles and in recognition of his place as one of Scotland's great 20th century authors.

We should like to thank Keith Sutherland for his unstinting support and assistance in the compilation of this book and Robin Smith of the National Library of Scotland for her courtesy and help.

1
Caithness and Sutherland

IN NEARLY ALL THE POPULAR guides to Scotland, Caithness is ignored or referred to as a place of little or no interest. I have beside me one of the best of them, *Scotland for Everyman,* where the author in his otherwise excellent and exact survey proceeds to warn the reader, as follows:

> East of Tongue the scenery rapidly decreases in grandeur as one gradually returns to civilization and tarred roads. Caithness is really rather a dull county, not Highland at all but rather Norse, at least near the coast – as the place-names show. Consequently the traveller will not be ill-advised if he decides to cut short this tour by making Lairg direct. If he does so, he will miss the kudos of having reached John o' Groats, but not very much else.

> This 'return to civilization' (after wandering in Sutherland) may have its points for a Caithness man, as there has always existed a certain rivalry – and raillery – between the two remotest counties of our mainland. But plainly he is not to be comforted by very much else. And as civilisation is a vague word and quite different in its implications from that other overworked word, culture, it might be said that the Sutherland man scores – particularly as some of his roads (including the famous old rocky highway to the Ord) have recently been tarred to perfection.

But the inwardness of this matter really centres in the use of that word grandeur. It is a legacy of Sir Walter Scott and all the Highland romanticism to which that noble name must plead guilty. Byron caught the note and sang it 'wild and majestic'.

Oh, for the crags that are wild and majestic!
The steep-frowning glories of dark Loch na Garr.

To see patriotic Scots roused by this gorgeous stuff is to realise in some measure the religious intensity of the old wife who would not believe that Jerusalem is on this earth. There is a magniloquence about it all, a lack of reality, of exact description, that flatters our vague emotions at the expense of our sight and insight. It is admirably reflected in those pictures for sale in stationers' shops where gigantic crags, their tops swathed in Celtic mist, form a background to smooth purple slopes and the wan water of a loch on whose near shores long-haired Highland cattle for ever stand and dream.

From all this, the curious reader may conclude that I am a Caithness man – preparing the way. He is right. The mind must be prepared for the reception of beauty in its more exquisite forms. The old man of the ceilidh-house realised this, and, before beginning one of the ancient classic poems of the Gael, he tuned the listening minds by telling of the poem itself and of its heroes. But he always followed with the poem. And now I am prepared to follow with two.

But as the Eastern sage has it, 'Haste is an attribute of devils'. Let us see one thing well; let us, then, as we turn east from Tongue, keep our eyes on Sutherland's own mountain – Ben Laoghal. Ben Hope comes before for contrast. And moors and sea-inlets and skylines keep us company. Around is all the grandeur of all the fabled West – with Ben Laoghal added. Watch Ben Laoghal play with its four granite peaks on the legendary stuff of history, or is it of the mind? Sometimes they are the battlemented towers of a distant Mediaeval Age; in the smoke-blue drift of the half-light they are the ramparts to the high hills of faery; a turn in the road or in the mood, and they have become perfectly normal again, unobtrusive and strong as the native character. Let me add that once going down towards bleak Kildonan, I unthinkingly glanced over my shoulder and saw them crowned with snow. I have never forgotten the unearthly fright I got then.

From that background, or as it were from that door, you walk out upon Caithness, and at once experience an austerity in the flat clean wind-swept lands that affects the mind almost with a sense of shock. There is something more in it than contrast. It is a movement of the spirit that finds in the austerity, because strength is there also, a final serenity. I know of no other landscape in Scotland that achieves this harmony, that, in the very moment of purging the mind of its dramatic grandeur, leaves it free and ennobled. The Pentland Firth, outreaching on the left, is of a blueness that I, at least, failed to find in the Mediterranean; a living blueness, cold-glittering in the sun and smashed to gleaming snowdrift on the bows of the great rock-battleships of the Orkneys, bare and austere also. The wind of time has searched out even the flaws here and cleansed them.

That is the first picture. Before we come to the second we follow the road by stone-flagged fences and broad fields to Thurso, a charming old town with a fishing-quarter of rather intricate design and a piling of roofs that, seen from the beach, has a certain attraction. From Thurso, like all good tourists we proceed to John o' Groats, so that we may sing about the end of the road. Picture postcards are here, and an hotel, and the legend of the house with the eight walls, the eight doors, and the eight-sided table, so that the eight men might enter and be seated without raising questions of precedence or prestige. But while listening to this local lore and, with luck, sampling the country's whisky – and old Pulteney, well matured, does no dishonour to its birthplace – we find our eyes attracted by that long lovely beach of white sand.

Not the poet's 'dove-grey sand', but the crushed shells of whiteness from which all the sticky humours have been withdrawn. It is in its way as typical of this clean-swept county as that first picture I have tried to describe. Hours may be spent on this strand looking for those lovely little shells, the John o' Groat buckies. In the process, too, the native spirit enters and quietens the soul.

But the leisureliness of an older age is gone. A look and a rush and we say we have seen it! The evening is upon us. Yet we have hardly got under way when from the low ridge of the Warth Hill, Caithness suddenly spreads her whole body before us to the blue distant ridges of Morven and the Scarabens.

This, my second picture, is impossible even to suggest, for the effect is entirely one of light. It is not that the quality of this light is magical or glamorous, tenuous or thin. There are few places in Scotland where level light from the sinking sun can come across such a great area; but it is not altogether that. Robert Louis Stevenson, who knew Wick well, may here have first found his 'wine-red moor', but I have seen it of a paler gold than amontillado. The mind does not debate: it gets caught up into that timelessness where beauty is no longer majestic or grand but something more intimate than life or death. Across the moor, the sun gone, the colour darkening, the far blue turning to deep purple, shadow and more shadow, until the peewits cry in the dark of night.

There is a third picture of Caithness but it is a composite one: the sea-cliffs that form its coast. In a sense, these cliffs are more typical of Caithness than all else for they have entered so much – and so violently – into the life of its people. As sheer rock-scenery, too, they are often magnificent, while the flatness of the coastlands permits of tremendous perspectives.

On entering the county from the Ord one may from almost anywhere near the cliffs get a view of the rock-wall all the way to Clyth Head. There are 'flaws' in this structure – fortunately, because they mean so much to the inhabitants, for here they have their harbours or creeks from which they fish with such skill and daring, or, should I say, have fished, for the decline in the sea industry has left an air of sadness and decay along the whole Caithness coast. In small places like Dunbeath or Lybster, where today only four or five motor-boats pursue the old calling, little more than a generation ago anything up to two hundred boats fished in the season from each harbour. What activity was there then! Every creek round the coast swarmed with life, while Wick, now going derelict, was a fishing-centre of European importance. Folk worked hard in those days, played hard, and drank hard, too. To live and prosper on such a coast required unusual intrepidity and endurance in the seamen. Few of the mean 'safe' qualities found time to sprout, and as the money came so did it go, with that element of careless generosity that is ever present in the greater games of chance. And sea-fishing is the master game of chance, for not only does a man risk all he possesses, with every grain of skill and strength added, but also he stakes down the hazard with his life. The fish-curers' stations employed as gutters nearly all the available women of the surrounding districts, whose gay tongues were as nimble as their fingers. Shopkeepers prospered. The produce of the land was needed. If there was never great wealth, there was all the living warmth of a healthy communal life.

When we look at the boarded windows of the ruinous curing buildings, we may naturally wonder what cataclysm or what blight descended here. The use of steam, the big drifter, the concentration of the industry in great ports like Wick, were the reasons given. But what of these reasons now? The drifter is in debt to more than a critical extent, and Wick is proportionately as derelict as Lybster.

Politics entered into it, and in a sense with far more drama than is usually found in the interactions of any 'economic law'. The export of cured herrings to the Baltic was lost when Russia began her social experiment. Not that Russia no longer required herrings, but that the British Government kept changing its mind about dealing with her. The herring is immensely more important to Scotland than to England. But Scotland could not deal separately in this matter. Norway, however, could and did. The Norwegian Government guaranteed Russian payments to the Norwegian fishermen to the extent of many millions of pounds. The Norwegian Government never lost a penny and the Norwegian fishermen got the market. It is interesting to reflect how the attitude of some politician seven hundred miles away may affect a seaboard and its people. Mr. Winston Churchill, let us say, decides on a little affair in Russia, and our northern coasts come under the grip of a grisly hand that slowly closes. They were such a fine breed of men, too, these Caithness fishermen, daring, self-reliant, rarely hypocritical or sanctimonious, game for whatever life offered in the sea-storm or in the public-house, and God-fearing over all.

Their qualities have been inherited, normal qualities of a healthy stock against an environment demanding courage and faith. Hospitality was the social gift, and the old need for quickness of wits may perhaps today find more or less a natural outlet in education. But whether the change from being skipper of a sailing vessel to being a school teacher, minister of the Gospel, clerk, professor, Civil Servant, or what-not, is a change for the better in the human story, may hardly be debated here. Personally, I am inclined to do more than doubt it.

All the coast is studded with castles mostly now in ruins and indicating an older age of tribal rule and self-sufficiency. Sinclairs, Keiths, Gunns; with Mackays, Sutherlands, and the ever land-hungry Campbells, impinging upon them from the outside. The tale of their deeds and depredations is as stormy and bloody and treacherous and heroic as tales from anywhere else in the Highlands. As a good-going example, may I be forgiven for recalling the ancient feud between the Keiths and the Gunns. The chiefs of these two clans agreed to settle their differences by a fight to the death of twelve men against twelve. The Gunn, with his chosen dozen, several of whom were his sons, was first at the lonely moorland rendezvous, and had barely ceased asking the Creator for His blessing, when the horses of the Keiths were seen to be approaching. Twelve horses behind the Keith, yes – but what is this? ... Each horse carries two riders! ... The Gunn puts it to his men. There is plenty of time to fly. But the Keith strategy, for some obscure reason, merely fires them to encounter any odds, and the battle is joined. It was a long and bloody affair, in which the Keiths claimed victory, but in the end three of the Gunns, albeit sorely wounded, were able to leave the field on their own feet.

A certain delicacy of feeling might well make a Gunn hesitate to tell the traditional story, were he not sadly aware that the clan did not know then – and certainly none of them has ever learned since – the technique of acquiring land or indeed notable material wealth of any kind. Nor from this story is any particular moral intended for our age, though I cannot help being conscious of a certain diffused light! We are landless! cried the Macgregors. And not only in the small clan of the Gunns, but in the large clan of the common people of Scotland, the cry has an intimate ring to this day.

These counties of Caithness and Sutherland may be said to have a pre-history of enthralling conjecture. Those interested in the archaeological aspect of things may here dream and dispute to their heart's content. Who built the brochs? – those round dwellings whose walls may still be seen from twelve to fifteen feet thick and whose original height must have been anything from fifty to sixty feet. They are structures of unique interest, crammed with novel features. The ruins of a great many of them are to be found in Caithness; rather less in Sutherland; and they diminish in number as we go south, until they become rare in the Lowlands. And perhaps the most remarkable fact about them is that they are to be found only in Scotland. Not a single example in Scandinavia, or Ireland, or England – those countries from which at one time or other Scotland is supposed to have got all she may be said to have! What race built them then? Was the seat of their power actually in the extreme north? Long ago Columba had to travel to Inverness to meet the high king of our country. Had the governing centre shifted south to Inverness by Columba's time, much as it later shifted to Edinburgh; and still later to London?

It is all a game of questions. But clearly in the courses of time these northern counties have had their day.

No writer can now refer to Caithness without using the word Norse. 'Not Highland at all but rather Norse.' A hundred odd years ago a traveller from the south would have had to penetrate into the county as far as Clyth before he could hear a word of English, no other tongue than Gaelic being spoken. True, you will find Norse coastal names; but you will also find them in the Outer Isles, where the Norse held sway just as long as they held it in Caithness. But they were conquerors, with the conqueror's technique of spoil-getting and land-grabbing. Their exploits are fabulous, and the only adventurers who can be compared with them are the Spanish Conquistadores. They were, however, few in numbers, were not of the soil they held, and in time the native folk of Caithness's hinterland, through their women, largely bred them out. That is not to say that Caithness folk are mostly Gaelic, any more than are other parts of the Highlands. There is an older more predominant strain in the Highlands than either Gaelic or Norse. What folk composed this strain I do not know, just as I do not know who built the brochs; but I have the uneasy idea that they rode one man to a horse.

All of which has brought us a little distance from the rock scenery. Not that the rock scenery is to blame, for it has beauty quite apart from its human associations. The geos and stacks and contorted strata, the colouring of caves and seaweed, the bird life, are elements of ever-varying allure. Memorable days maybe passed haunting this world that swings between life and death. Great care should be taken, too, for on a windless sea where no waves are breaking there is always some degree of a swell that may all in a moment lift a small boat on to a sloping ledge and, receding, leave her to turn turtle.

For the rest, Caithness is said to be a flat treeless plain, and perhaps that impression may have been confirmed here; yet like so many general impressions it is only partially true. For Caithness has many shallow straths of delicate beauty, that penetrate inland from the coast and fade into the moor with an air of still, listening surprise. The Strath of Dunbeath is considered to be about the finest example, though I have found Berriedale and Langwell of inexhaustible attraction. There are others, many of them not at all impressive to the casual eye, that yet achieve for the lover an intimacy and charm that may be comparable only to the fragrance of the finer wines.

Possibly I am prejudiced in favour of Caithness, knowing, as I do, that it possesses qualities which, like the qualities of its people, are not readily paraded. Yet let me say immediately that had Caithness denied me, I should have desired, over any other place on the earth's surface (including the vineyard countries), to have been born in Sutherland!

Caithness and Sutherland are, in a way not easily made plain, a mating of the two great elements of sea and land. You can get lost in Sutherland, in its mountain masses, its great glens, its hidden lochs, its peat hags, its woods, its barren moors. It is shaggy and tough and often terrifying. The eye reaches over great vistas where no human being lives or moves. And on the west the traveller finds himself for ever playing a game of hide and seek with the sea. Narrow inlets meet him round corners, sudden flashes of colour drawing his eyes away. The memory of a trip from Scourie northward is curiously jewelled. The greenness of mountains where one had expected to find heather, the land between mountain and sea assuming every shape, fantastic, ancient, grey, brooding in peat black, glistening in loch blue, unexpected in goblin green, dreaming in brown, the wind touching it, passing over it, carrying away its loneliness to some place still more deeply withdrawn. To think of the Caithness coast now is to think of something simple, elemental, masculine. Here is the beauty of ceaseless change, full of a wild charm, alluring, beckoning, heedless, feminine.

Sutherland has always been a pastoral crofting county and the tragedy it suffered in the beginning of last century may best be realised if from Caithness we go 'over the Ord' by the south coast road and come down upon the fishing town of Helmsdale.

Helmsdale, like the Caithness creeks, has fallen on evil times these latter years. But its story is interesting in that it was a direct creation of what is known to history as the 'Sutherland Clearances'. These clearances consisted in the evictions of thousands of crofters from their homes in the glens by a landlord who desired, for his greater profit, to rent his land to sheep farmers. It was the era throughout the whole Highlands of the creation of the large sheep farm, and of the dispossession of the people, frequently by means so ruthless and brutal that they may not bear retelling easily, and always with a sorrow and hopelessness that finally broke the Gaelic spirit. What the disaster of 1745 and the penal enactments of 1747 began, the clearances finished.

We know rather exactly and vividly what happened in the glens of Sutherland because of the accounts of eye-witnesses and the explanations of contemporaries. Donald Macleod, whose wife and family were evicted into a night of storm when he himself was absent, with no neighbour they dare go to without bringing immediate doom to that neighbour's house, described the lurid scenes of burning

8

and destruction in a series of letters to an Edinburgh newspaper, afterwards printed in book form under the title *The Gloomy Memories*. These letters make terrible reading. The Rev Donald Sage, in his *Memorabilia Domestica*, tells of the hundreds of homes that were burned around him and of how, when he came to preach his last sermon, he broke down and all his people wept with him. For untold generations they and their forebears had inhabited these glens, a courteous people, hospitable, full of the ancient lore and music and ways of life of the Gael and the pre-Gael. No army of invading barbarians ever left behind it desolation so complete as did that ruthless handful of the chief's servants. And Sutherland to this day is haunted by that 'gloomy memory'.

The folk gathered on the seashores, eating shellfish or whatever they could find, while they dug small plots of coastal land and tackled the sea. Helmsdale gradually became a fishing port of consequence. Then Helmsdale declined, as the sheep farms declined, and the great experiment in Progress had its mask torn from it.

From Helmsdale the traveller should take the road that goes up Kildonan strath, over the Heights, and down Strath Halladale to Melvich on the north coast, both for the scenery and to experience, as I think he may, a still lingering intimation of that gloom. For this is the area that, with Strath Naver farther west, suffered most cruelly.

And the first reaction may well be one of surprise that a land so barren and wild could ever have harboured townships of people. How did they manage to live? … Until finally he may wonder if the 'clearances' would not have happened sometime anyway.

The further north he goes the bleaker it gets until crossing the high lands he observes little but endless desolation. Then all at once he comes on Dalhalvaig.

In Dalhalvaig there is a public school, a post office, substantial houses on the surrounding crofts, white-washed walls, an air of comfort, of material well-being, of everything, in fact, except that which suggests poverty and misery. Yet half-close the eyes, let the houses disappear, let the heather creep up to the hearth-stones, let all sign of human habitation vanish, and the present Dalhalvaig becomes a place more desolate than any to be found in Kildonan.

How do we account, then, for the Dalhalvaig of today? On no other grounds that I can think of than that Strath Halladale was not 'cleared'. It escaped the horrors of 1813-19 because the greater part of it was at that time under the Mackays, and when it did fall into other hands (in 1829, by purchase) public feeling against the evictions had got so inflamed that the new owners found it more advantageous to pursue the intriguing ways of Parliamentary influence than to continue making deserts.

Down the Strath from Forsinard to the sea the descendants of the old crofters remained. Many of them caught the emigration fever as the nineteenth century advanced and went abroad meaning to return, but few of them ever returned to settle, though they sent home money regularly and in other ways exhibited the passion of the Gael for his homeland and his kindred.

In talk and correspondence with the present scholarly parish minister of Kildonan I have been given a glimpse of the kind of men and women Dalhalvaig has produced not only in the past but in living memory. 'Some of the finest types of Northern Highlander, physically and mentally, have come out of this area from Kirkton to Forsinain on both sides of the Halladale river', Dr Scott maintains, And he proves his case with fascinating instances of versatility, strong personality, and occasional genius.

I was interested in this contrast between Kildonan and Halladale, and pursued my inquiries quite dispassionately. I think there is here an underlying significance of real importance. A great human stock cannot be planted in a day. What was uprooted so swiftly may not all at once be given root and permanence by a decision of any individual or any Board. But the glens are there. And the final – and representative – opinion was given me in these words: 'All the northern glens might have been like Halladale, if the people had been treated as human beings.'

But this is a depressing subject and for all that may have been written to the contrary, the Highlander loves news and gaiety. As Kenneth Macleod reports of the island schoolmaster, 'My curse on gloom!' Only it is necessary to get some understanding of the forces, human and economic, that have been doing him down in the past in order to appreciate even the scenery amid which he lives now. For not only does environment affect human development, but human development in its turn affects environment. In a happy thriving community the very land, to our senses, takes on a certain pleasant friendliness. Children feel this particularly, and in after life have an enhanced memory of sunlight and of flowering growths. On the other hand, in Kildonan there is today a shadow, a chill, of which any sensitive mind would, I am convinced, be vaguely aware, though possessing no knowledge of the clearances. We are affected strangely by any place from which the tide of life has ebbed.

And Sutherland, as I have suggested, is a land of endless variety. There are no big towns, nothing at all like Wick, which in the height of the herring season in the old days used to double its population and present a scene of human interest continuously dramatic. The county town of Dornoch is best known for its golf course. Golspie and Brora also have good golf courses. Here a tourist industry is developing. And as this part of the county is also the seat of landlord power, there is a certain residential feeling in the atmosphere. Surrounding the castle are fields with trees like English parks, while on a high hill dominating all this part of the coast is a tall monument to that Duke of Sutherland under whose reign the clearances took place.

Let us go inland to Lairg, which is the proper centre for the exploration of the real Sutherland. Anything in the nature of motor-car or bus service may be had at the Sutherland Transport garage, where a genial manager, in Gaelic or English, will tell you what you want to know and what you had not thought of. Three main roads radiate from Lairg to the west. The first up the quietly beautiful strath of the Oykel to Lochinver; the second by the long barren stretches of Loch Shin to Scourie; and the third northward across the moors, passing the Clibric Hills on the right, to Tongue. All three roads run into the road of the west which winds from Lochinver to Tongue, and is, to me at least, literally the most surprising and magical road in Britain. Not that speedmen would call it a road at all, unless indeed certain parts might be selected for 'observing'.

Through Strath Oykell, by Altnagealgach, and on towards Loch Assynt, where great mountains all at once crowd around: Ben More Assynt (3,273 ft.) on our right; Canisp and the remarkable Suilven on our left; Glasven and the Quinag in front. This is the happy hunting-ground of geologists, archaeologists, and botanists. Historians, too, will look at the ruins of Ardvreck Castle on the edge of Loch Assynt and think of Montrose and what happened there of 'deathless shame'.

From Lochinver, a pleasant place, there is a coast road by Clashnessie and Drumbeg to Kylescue Ferry (for Scourie) that no summer traveller should miss. It is not much frequented, but I have always found a great fascination in the wooded inlets that give on Eddrachillis Bay, with its many islands.

Islands, indeed, accompany one along this western seaboard, and exercise their power on the romantic imagination in diverse ways. Some look upon them quiescently, others dreamily with vague thoughts of Tir nan Og, while not a few feel an impulse to own one doubtless out of some innate urge for security and over-lordship. All hopes – or illusions – may be indulged on this road. Life is short, but eternity may be dreamed in a minute.

From Scourie to Laxford Bridge, where the Loch Shin road ends or begins. All this is sporting country. The Laxford River has patrol paths on both sides, and I have heard of young men who strike a match in the dark of night by this lonely water and then wait to see how long it will take keepers to come out of the void upon them! A remarkably short time, I am told. Whether or not it has its point as a game, it certainly illustrates with some irony the whole subject of sporting rights on which I have not touched here. It is really difficult to write of the Highlands without appearing to deal in that accursed gloom. When the sheep did not pay, the deer took their place. I may leave it at that. As for getting a rod on the Laxford, you would first have to buy out the wealthiest duke in England. So you may leave it at that also!

The hotels have, of course, some loch-fishing attached to them. It is the custom, I know, to deplore the heavy charges – six to eight guineas a week – of most of them. But their season is short, their rent and expenses heavy, and they desire profit as naturally as a duke or a grocer. For the rest, they know their business. The Highlands, of course, may yet become a popular tourist playground dependent on tourists and nothing else. After sheep, deer; and after deer, tourists. It is the ascending order of our age of progress. For those who know the deep humanism of a past age, there will be regret at the gradual passing of the human stock that was bred of it.

But by the time a man has footed the track to Cape Wrath, where there is no habitation other than the lighthouse, and looked down upon the rocks that take the Arctic on their bows, he may feel that men's faiths or creeds, economic or religious, change with the centuries, that his wants and desires change with the days, but that certain deep racial forces persist with extra-ordinary strength, and that the end of this great country is not yet.

2

East to Buchan

'WE ARE COMING UP TO Inverness for a day or two. Can you recommend some outings that would give us an idea of the far north of which we have heard so much?'

That is a typical inquiry, and the easy answer takes the roads to the west, by Garve and Achnasheen to Loch Maree and Gairloch, or right through to Lairg and then by Loch Shin to Scourie, Cape Wrath, Durness and the north road to Caithness. You never make a mistake if you send a traveller into those regions, for the appeal of the scenery is immediate; and indeed it is very beautiful.

But there is another road that I am sometimes tempted to send a discerning friend, though I try to make sure first of all that he cares for two things: the sea itself and the way of life of those who draw their livelihood exclusively from the sea. Once assured on these points, I suggest the coast road along the southern shores of the Moray Firth 'east to Buchan'.

For the normal traveller in our country, this remains an unknown region, because it is so rarely written or spoken about. Yet what a fascination it can have for landsmen who care to linger about the fishing villages and see and attempt to understand the strange ways of life that are here so quietly followed!

The other night I spent with a friend who has entered into possession of a fisherman's cottage that overlooks one of the harbour basins of Macduff. He is an artist and writer, of a distinguished sea ancestry, who knows the seamen of Brittany or Italy as well as he knows those of the English Channel, but who has come to live here from choice. And after spending a couple of days with him, I may put it mildly by saying that I see his point! For no one can 'retire' to a small fishing-port, in the sense that he may sit down and fold his hands and let the days go by. There is always too much going on, or about to go on, or held up – according to the weather or the season of the year. For this traffic with the sea is essentially in the nature of a continuous gamble, a gamble in material results, but also a gamble not infrequently with life or death where the winning counters are knowledge and endurance and courage – and these counters do not always win.

The distinguishing feature of the fishing villages along this coast is the cleanliness of the houses, not merely inside but also outside. You can see they are seamen's houses, for they are all shipshape and bright with paint. Macduff is no exception, and when you turn and look at it from the harbour wall, it stands against its uprising green brae like a little town that one might come upon in a southern land – at some distance, let us say, for Macduff's appearance of solidity and brightness stands the closest inspection.

They are very go-ahead in Macduff: at a short distance they have constructed a splendid bathing-pool, and on the hillside above it there is a golf-course. It is not unknown for a woman to be seen baiting her husband's sea-lines in the morning and to be golfing in the afternoon. Which is surely one of the first and best of any reasons for the existence of a golf-course. Macduff is not – as yet, anyway – a fashionable resort. For the most part, the visitors who come here are workers who have earned their short holiday and live in the houses of the people, with whom they make friends. The real old Scots democratic feeling and no nonsense.

At six o'clock in the morning we were on the quay seeing the handful of drifters coming in with, as it happened, their very small shots of herring, which were auctioned on the spot. Here are one or two women with their barrows, trundling away baskets of herring to be used as bait for the small lines, which later in the day will be taken to sea by the smaller boats engaged in the white fishing. My friend is given a fry of herring – and presents them to me. To get the real flavour of almost any sea fish, you must eat it the day it is caught. A lemon sole fresh from the sea has a salty tang that I have never got in any city hotel.

The town of Banff lies across the bay, but no fishing is carried on there now. At one time Banff was a very important seaport, as well as a social centre for the country, but the high stores by the harbour are derelict and the slipway is empty.

The ruins of crofting houses in the glens can be a sad enough sight, but they do not convey to me so immediate a feeling of desolation as do the boarded-up windows of cooperages, the grass-grown yards and crumbling stores of these fishing villages all along the Moray Firth that once knew so busy, so thrilling a life.

Beyond Banff, we dropped down into the fishing village of Whitehills that still lives on the sea. The fishermen were putting their small lines aboard. Some ten lines to each boat, and each line with five hundred hooks, baited with herring. It's a saying that there mustn't be a lazy inch in a fisherman – or in his wife. Whitehills is in many respects typical of the small sea villages along this coast. Usually the road, from the wide plain above, drops very steeply, and the village is come upon suddenly and conveys the air of being shut away from the world. In such a place, the houses have generally their gables to the sea, and group together as if for comfort and warmth. Which is understandable and wise enough, when one reflects that it might be unskilled advice to suggest to these seamen and often anxious women that they should build to have a 'good view' of the sea! The sea is always with them, and when a storm is blowing up it's not a bad thing to be shut away from it, even if the 'view' is then no more than the back wall of a neighbour's house. At least that wall is stable – even though it doesn't shut out the unending roar.

To paint a solid stone cottage all blue may seem as absurd as to paint it all pink. But when you see the blue cottage and the pink cottage there is no absurdity, but on the contrary a pleasant surprise that they should look so well. They paint their houses as they paint their boats. This indeed is the most striking characteristic of all the dwellings along this coast. The cottage may be painted blue, but each stone is picked out in straight white lines. Though there again it is a matter of shade or tone. And this contrasting of colours on the one house, they have brought to a careful art. Yellows, blues, greys, dark reds passing into maroon. Mostly, of course, the whole wall is not painted, though there is a soft dark-blue stone that loses nothing by being enclosed within narrow white lines. And some of the red fluted tiles are tarred black and look ancient and very well. The tar preserves the tile. The individualism of the Scot comes out, too, in the case, say, of two dwellings in the one building (semi-detached), where each has its own colour scheme, as if the houses want to show that they need not necessarily be on speaking terms.

It was raining heavily when we crossed the Bridge of Banff, heading for Buchan along the coast road. This road is as surprising as the villages, for surely along the flat plain of Buchan the road should be fairly level and for the most part straight. Actually the road turns and twists as continuously as it goes up and down. One expects – and finds – the usual dangerously steep gradient going down into the very attractive fishing village of Pennan, but once more up on the plain one may be forgiven for almost stalling when, a short distance further on, one encounters a sudden incline which at the turn to the top must be pretty nearly 1-in-4. These twists and declivities are caused by the little green valleys that are always finding their way to the sea. Intimate valleys, with the wind whitening the bracken on their green braes.

The sun came out through the watery skies and opened up and brightened the mist-shrouded land, and in that fresh, warm light Buchan was anything but the cold, bleak region that a traveller may expect. Large bien farms here, and comfortable steadings, and inland the slow austere sweep of the land. A good, sound, strong country. Up over the rise of a field in the lifting brilliant mist came a ploughman behind his horse, a great beast stepping quickly and proudly against the gradient and the pull of the scuffler behind. And there the picture was complete: the sea and the land. The man who harvests the sea and the man who harvests the land. In a last resort we can do without all others: kings, emperors, political leaders, financiers, merchant princes, moderators, artists, writers and all. For in any age the folk of the land and sea have never failed to produce their own writers or ballad-makers, their own poets, just as they have never failed to produce their own artists in paint and stone. But for those others – in the final count they can be forgotten and perhaps even forgiven.

The advent of steam, of the steam drifter, drained the living power from innumerable fishing villages on the Moray Firth into the big ports of Wick, Fraserburgh and Peterhead, and as we now approached Fraserburgh this became increasingly evident. but before we entered Fraserburgh we came upon an extraordinary sight, that was surely a portent and a sign: a cemetery of drifters. It was as if a fleet of them, like a school of enormous whales, had run themselves aground, become permanently stranded, and rotted. From some the planking was entirely gone, leaving the gaunt ribs for wind and salt spray to whistle through. They had all taken the ground head-on, some had slewed round, at least one had broken its back. It seemed a tragic end to a story that in every case had been charged with danger and courage, hope and despair, continuous vigilance, ceaseless adventure, in summer seas, in winter's smashing storms. If each skeleton could tell its true story, and tell the stories, too, of those who had walked its decks and of those who waited on shore for a return that brought the welcome news of safety first and of plenty or poverty next, this bay, this cemetery, would be the birth-place of an imperishable epic. Each boat had been deliberately stranded. When a skipper-owner walks away for the last time from a vessel that he has sailed on the right side of death for thirty years, a vessel that he and his crew and their families have depended on, through good fortune and bad, what a parting must be there! Perhaps only those who deal with the sea can understand.

Fraserburgh was in the thick of the summer herring fishing, and drifters were continuously arriving as we walked about the quays. But herring were scarce. A few crans were the order of the day – and a few crans are not enough to earn the £60 a week that one skipper told me were needed to keep things going. These drifters are in a bad way, and the banks know it. A skipper-owner, pointing to his drifter, said he had offered her in full commission to his banker as security for a loan of £50, and his banker had refused the loan. Another suggested that the days of the drifter are numbered. He cast his eyes over the scores of vessels about him, as they crowded in, nose to the quay, and remarked: 'Not one of them is under twenty years old'. One could feel the air of gloom all along the quays. Most of these quiet, hardy men had known the port in the old sailing days. One intelligent skipper's verdict: 'Things in the port are better organised now, but times are not so good.' Which was rather a terrible comment on what we call progress.

Peterhead, swarming with drifters from ports as far apart as Buckie and Lowestoft, presented the same state of affairs. Old drifters and remorseless debt – making one think back to that portentous sea-cemetery. Yet the tenacious seamen fight on. One or two good shots, and their spirits rise again and hope is renewed. They are a great race.

I got the impression, too, of a spirit abroad in Peterhead that is not going to take defeat easily. Some of the keenest minds have begun to understand that the final value of a sea's harvesting may rest not entirely in the realm of economics but more and more in the realm of politics. They see what foreign governments have been able to do for their fisheries. They are asking shrewd questions – and are likely to go on asking them. One wise old worker on the quays began to explain how and why the industry had never gone ahead in organising new selling methods, as all other great industries had done. For fifteen years, he said, he had been advocating such a simple thing as the packing of cured herrings in small, round tin boxes, but no one would take the matter up. Who wants to buy half a barrel at a time? And I must say I think he is quite right. If one cannot get a few cured herrings at a time – one buys none at all.

But this is not an economic essay. It is no more than a suggestion that there are many ways of spending a touring holiday and that there are more things to look at than mountains in this old heroic northern land of ours.

3
My Bit of Britain

To one who has wandered about the Highlands of Scotland most of his life, it is difficult all in a moment to say, 'This is my favourite bit.' After a long spell on the East Coast, to go by Invermoriston and Loch Cluanie to the shores of Loch Duich is to emerge into a new world that the blood knows as immemorially old. On the treeless plain of Caithness, one can see the pines in the gorge on the way to Gairloch; by the gaunt rock-bound shores of the north-east, the islands and anchorages in the Western Ocean. Once in a reckless moment I bought a boat, and, with the help of Admiralty charts and the grace of God, we navigated her – my wife and I – along much of that western seaboard during summer months of distinctly varied weather. It was an experience to dream about. We often do.

Perhaps the deciding factor in this matter of choice is an irrational one, irrational in the sense that it has little to do with any scheme of preference involving explicit aesthetic or material considerations. This is my corner of the Highlands, here my earliest memories were formed, and so, for better or for worse, richer or poorer, I stick by it. It is the way the blood argues. And in itself it is perhaps not a bad way, for it springs out of affection and loyalty. All the theorists who argue so nobly against nationalism and for peace miss this simple point, it seems to me. When the blood fondly says 'This is my land,' it is at that moment profoundly in harmony and at peace. When it cannot say that, something has gone wrong, and it is that something that is the evil thing. Not, of course, that I think my bit is inferior to any other in its variety of natural feature and attractiveness! The country that lies around the borders of the counties of Caithness and Sutherland provides, in fact, more striking scenic contrasts than I have found elsewhere throughout our island. Approaching Caithness along the north road, you leave behind a land of heather and mountain, the great mass of Ben Hope, the airy granite peaks of Ben Laoghal, and then suddenly the eye encounters the vast rolling plain of Caithness. Behind is a memory of little croft houses backed by heather; in front are farms whose fences are upended flagstones, whose very pattern seems bare, rectangular, austere, like certain modernist pictures. With the sun in the south – and despite southern opinion it does shine quite often in this northland – the waters of the Pentland Firth take on a vivid brilliant blue, and in this blue the Orkneys lie at anchor like fabulous battleships. Here lived the ancient native Pict, and hither came the Gaelic missionary to woo him from his Druidism, and the Viking raider to despoil him of land and life.

Those of us who live, or have lived, in cities, and know modern industrialism in all its phases, may justly feel some impatience at useless echoes of battles long ago. But this northland is not an industrial area and must live as best it can amid its own influences. When I was a boy, that unique circular edifice called a broch was one corner of a wide playground. I say unique because it is unknown outside Scotland, and, inside Scotland, Caithness has the greatest number. They are now ruins, of course – some of them were ruins overgrown with moss when the Vikings came in the eighth or ninth century – but our ruin still had its beehive chamber intact in the twelve-foot thick wall. There we admired the cunning masonry, cut our names on the stone, or dug up shells of edible shellfish.

The south road to this area skirts the shores of the North Sea until it runs into the fishing creek of Helmsdale, the outlet of the Strath of Kildonan. Thence it climbs steeply, in great hairpin loops round ravines, to the Ord of Caithness, where the sea cliffs are over 600 feet high. From this elevated primeval moorland, where no habitation is, the coastline is seen as a continuous wall of rock to distant Clyth Ness. Actually there are a few short gaps in this wall, and each is – or was – a fishing creek. Indeed, if we are interested in the lives of a people, in economic issues, we have here before us a perfect example of the beginning, rise, and fall of a very great industry, all within a century, last century.

When we look at the sea off our coasts it is normally impossible to tell which way the tide is running, it is even difficult to tell whether the tide is flowing or ebbing without studying the actual beach at our feet for some time. But in the Pentland Firth you can see the tidal stream running east or west, you can see its beginnings, its increase, its height, when it is like a gigantic and turbulent river, its decline and fall to slack water. In cities or industrial areas it may be difficult to say with certainty how the economic current is flowing, but here on the Caithness coast a whole tidal process in economics can be studied from beginning to end.

It is a remarkable story. Early in last century the Government decided that the herring fisheries along our coasts – hitherto a monopoly of the Dutch – should be nationally encouraged, and with that object in view offered to pay a bounty of at first two shillings and then four on every barrel of herring cured. Round about the time Napoleon was being convoyed to St. Helena, the herring tide set in along these northern shores. Every kind of craft was pressed into service, local boat-building was, as we now say, geared to an ever increasing output, coopers were trained, curing yards built, women and girls of the crofts became expert gutters and packers, and soon there was discernible that hectic movement of life we associate with a gold rush. In 1830 the bounties were dropped, but by then nothing could stop the progress of the industry and it took the loss of the bounties in its stride. Schooners appeared to carry the barrels to distant lands. The Baltic markets in particular became a northern gold mine. From these creeks in that rock wall – Helmsdale, Dunbeath, Lybster, Clyth – hundreds of boats were fishing. The boats increased in size, grew in numbers. As time went on, they took in the West Coast fishing, the season at the Shetlands, at Fraserburgh and Peterhead, and finally set sail for East Anglia. Then came steam, the large ports with docking facilities and unlimited capital, and the golden age of the creeks began to decline. By the early years of this century, they were derelict.

One more economic note and the living pattern of this region in recent generations may be seen. For what immediately preceded, and for some time coincided with, the growth of the herring fisheries pertained to the land and was as horrible in destruction as the rise of the fisheries was remarkable in construction. This was the movement by the great landlords of clearing the crofters out of the glens in order to make room for sheep. In that area which goes up the Strath of Kildonan from Helmsdale and on to the Pentland Firth some 15,000 crofters were dispossessed and driven from their homes, often in circumstances of brutality. Great numbers of them were shipped abroad, but many joined the fishing communities on the coast, and their descendants today, as in the last war, man our mine-sweepers and fighting craft, for where expert seamanship and individual initiative are needed, there they are naturally found.

So in this far northland, if we may not know much of the life of cities and industrial areas, we know all right what the struggle for existence means. The land and the sea, the produce of earth and ocean: these have been the concern of the folk who live on the crofts and in the fishing villages. They bred a fine tough type when the going was good; daring men, willing to lay hands on opportunity, prepared to face anything, quietly religious.

With the coming of the motor-engined fishing boat, around forty-feet keel, there has been a small stirring of life in some of the creeks. But whether this seaboard will ever again see the tumultuous life it once knew is another matter. Some of us have our theories, but optimism is not a quality that finds over-ready houseroom here where men and women have known what struggle means.

Between the two seas is a vast hinterland of mountain, moor, and glen, given over to sheep, grouse, and deer, for the vast bulk of the folk live by or near the sea. It is good sporting country, and many a happy day I have spent in its wilds. As I write, one holiday in particular comes back to mind. I owned at the time a small saloon car whose seats were so arranged that in a couple of minutes they could be extended into two beds. There are many ways of sleeping out. I have done it in an old bothy, under a strip of canvas, or openly in the heather without any covering (this last way would be as good as any, did not the midges delight in tangling themselves in your hair). But for the comfort that is perfect, I have never known anything to equal that little saloon car. After an exhausting expedition on foot, to return and eat, to put up a fishing rod and get a few trout in the evening, to have a last stroll to some particular eminence or hollow, to wander back and, while the beds are being prepared, to get some fresh water in the kettle, to undress and get into bed, to pour out two drinks for careful dilution from the kettle's spout, to light a last cigarette, to lie back and watch the night come in and around in a slow quietude, is to know why man needed and so created the word 'magic.'

We were in the heart of a deer forest, many miles from the nearest house, which was a stalker's. We had neither rifle nor gun and so got on terms of intimacy with the wild life of the region. We could, for example, look at a young mountain hare and say, 'His top speed *is* 26 m.p.h.,' for we occasionally did a long cruise for milk and bread and so could test such matters, as no hare would leave the road in front until he came to his own home path, not though we almost sat on his tail. Sometimes, in a ground mist, for fear of running him down, I would stop the car. But presently we would come on him again, for he had rested as we had rested, and then, with one ear forward and one aft, he would show us his paces once more. In this way one seemed to get a sort of intuitive knowledge of the home or social life of the hare. But the social life of the deer had now and then a fascination which will not attempt to describe. For we were no students of wild life. We were there to enjoy what we saw, not only in wild life, but in the shapes of hills and corries and moors, in loch and stream, and, over all, in the ever-varying effects of sun and shadow and mist and small rain. But that hour of summer twilight, when all our world grew quiet, gathered all the hours into it, as a man's life is gathered in his thought. For the rest, let it be said that we did have a particular interest (for such an interest gives cohesion to a holiday) – my wife in what plant life could be found, and myself in the sources of one or two streams.

Physically the two counties are divided by a range of hills which, though not very high (Morven, 2,313ft. is the highest peak) are made particularly prominent by the general flatness of Caithness. There is a road that runs from Latheron on the North Sea to Thurso on the Pentland Firth across some twenty-five miles of moorland, from which this range looks in certain lights like a vast bastion of mountain. But the quality of the light on the Caithness moors is sometimes of an extraordinary fineness. It is not altogether a matter of great distances, for I know the moor of Rannoch at all hours, and have looked over wide enough vistas in some Continental countries. Perhaps the clear air of these northern latitudes and the surrounding seas may have something to do with it – not to mention the effect of countless square miles of ling turned to pale gold.

But this land, which guide books ignore, beyond a reference to bare, treeless, and uninteresting, has its intimate beauty in its little glens or straths. Scenery in the public sense has its fashions, of course, and some of us are not impressed unless the mountains rear perilously overhead and the glens are deep as Gehenna. We must be shocked into taking notice. Even death must be on a colossal scale before we are impressed. But as an intimate affair, death, like life and like beauty, is individual and personal. The death of a true friend still touches us more nearly than the death of a thousand strangers. If it doesn't, something is going wrong.

These small straths, like the Strath of Dunbeath, have this intimate beauty. In boyhood we get to know every square yard of it. We encompass it physically and our memories hold it. Birches, hazel trees for nutting, pools with trout and an occasionally visible salmon, river-flats with the wind on the bracken and disappearing rabbit scuts, a wealth of wild flower and small bird life, the soaring hawk, the unexpected roe, the ancient graveyard, thoughts of the folk who once lived far inland in straths and hollows, the past and the present held in a moment of day-dream.

There may be a lot of nostalgia in the Canadian boatman's longing for the 'lone shieling' and the 'misty island,' but at least it springs from memories that had once held this intimacy and beauty, in moments beyond the hazards and struggles of life, and would experience it again if it could.

4

One Fisher Went Sailing
The Plight of the West Coast Herring Ports

For weeks we have been cruising down the West Coast of Scotland in our small boat, and if our personal adventures have been many and exciting, there has been one constant factor in our experience, and that is the poverty of the sea-fishing. We had anticipated no difficulty in catching white fish of all kinds: we found that apart from being unable to catch fish ourselves, though we had most of the usual lures, and used all sorts of bait from mussels to crushed partan, we were unable to buy fresh fish, except in the towns of Tobermory and Oban – and there the fish was not locally caught but came from distant cities.

I am aware that this, to dwellers on the East Coast, may seem an exaggeration, for where are there finer fishing banks in the world, both for quality and quantity, than on the West Coast of Scotland, with its innumerable inlets and bays, its sands for flat fish, its rocks – a glance at an Admiralty chart should be enough to frighten any but the most foolhardy amateur navigator – for lobsters, and its endless variety of bottom-feeding for the usual marketable white fish? Yet I am stating no more than a fact from personal experience, and when I cast back carefully through that experience, I find myself hesitating over only one modifying instance, and that occurred in Iona, where we got kippers from Stornoway, and, being McIver's kippers, they were first-class.

We did come on one small kippering station on the mainland, where the herring were gutted and cleaned by a rather marvellous machine, but after that they were not smoked but dyed in vats, and we were sufficiently prejudiced in favour of the smoked kipper, with its crisp flavour, not to care for this dyed article of commerce, however brown and pretty it might look. It was shortly afterwards that we saw something of the controversy in the press on this subject, arising out of statements made in the House of Commons by the Member for Argyll, and though our sympathies are flagrantly in favour of any system of herring cure that will ensure a popular sale and thereby assist the fishermen, yet after taking every factor into consideration we were inclined to support the Member for Argyll, and for this overriding reason, that in the long run it is the best type of article that pays, and by that we mean the most palatable and wholesome. The trouble so often with the smoked kipper as exposed for sale in our shops is that it was not a herring in really prime condition to begin with. A housewife can tell this at once by its thin, watery taste. After having had bad luck once or twice in her purchases, she simply stops buying. It is possible that the dyeing process may conceal lack of quality to some extent by keeping the flesh apparently more moist and full of oil, thereby ensuring readier sale to the poor or the indiscriminating: but at the back of this there is the undoubted fact – as in the case of these Stornoway kippers we got in Iona – that a sound herring, properly cured by smoke, is the most palatable form of the kipper, and therefore the most likely in the long run to win a steady and increasing market. Those we got were so delicious that we boiled some of them, and the flesh came away from the bone as it does from the bone of a prime finnan haddie.

But we got them only once, and we were never lucky enough to find any fresh herring at all. The West Coast season has so far (I write in the first days of August) been a complete failure. At Mallaig we saw a couple of drifters when we should have seen fifty. In Oban we were saddened by the spectacle of herring curing stations overgrown with grass and cooperages dilapidated, a scene all too familiar to us in so many of the Moray Firth fishing creeks. A fish salesman gave it to me as his opinion that Oban as a herring port is finished.

'But what if a late herring season comes along on the West?' I asked.

'Make no difference', he answered. 'Mallaig and Castlebay will handle it easy – particularly so far as the Scottish boats are concerned.' I asked him what he meant by that. 'The Scottish boats are so much in debt that they can't fit out for a late fishing – very few of them, anyway.'

It was the answer I had expected. I asked him if the Herring Industry Board's report was out. In the same laconic voice he said it was. Later, in the press, I read extracts from it and recognised it as the most desperate document yet issued on the subject, amounting in pith to little more than a statement endeavouring, by the aid of analytical reason, to show the inevitability of the early death of the whole Scottish herring fishing industry based on the system of the family boat. As far as I could see, there was not one constructive suggestion in it.

Meantime, standing on the quay at Oban, where two trawlers were unloading and a third manoeuvring for a berth, I asked the fish salesman how it was that we could not catch fish on the West. As he looked at the trawlers, a dry expression came into his face. I could not help smiling at this silent comment, for the depredations of these trawlers on the inshore banks had been mentioned to me by fishermen everywhere. Now, though I knew the trawlers could clean up a fishing bank pretty thoroughly if they got half a chance, yet I was not disposed to blame them altogether. Let me put it mildly by saying that the West Coast does tend to breed a natural inertia. If one has food today, tomorrow is soon enough to try to get some more: and if one has cash to buy fish from Glasgow, why worry at all about catching them? Moreover, I had got a pretty thorough insight into the operation of unemployment benefit or the dole on the West, and more particularly in the Islands, where occasional instances of what is termed 'faked employment' have attained the perfection of an art. But I cannot begin to go into this here without appearing to misrepresent those who draw benefit – and to do as much would not only be unjust but stupid, for we are now discussing an Act framed for industrial areas and completely inapplicable to the conditions of life and work in the Highlands and Islands. I can sympathise with the Scottish Office in the task it has in front of it – and even more with the man who can achieve the certainty of the dole over against the tempestuous uncertainty of catching fish that no longer appear to exist!

What the outcome of all this is going to be is another matter. From my own investigations, I can see no outcome, if the present conditions continue, but the end of the old Highland life and polity as we have known it, and in its place a sporting landlordism and tourism all complete. I do not write this lightly. But neither may I avoid the facts, encountered everywhere, of depopulation, of disappearing crofts, of half ruinous fishing villages, of young men refusing to go to sea – except as deck hands on summer yachts or trading vessels. I know of places where the young men not only do not know how to handle boats and to fish, but – more deadly even – do not know where the fishing banks are, a knowledge dying with the old.

So I come back to these trawlers at Oban and wonder if they have helped this decline in some measure.

'How much fish have they landed today?' I asked.

'I don't know today's figures but on Monday they landed 2,600 boxes. Some days it's less.'

For one small quay it seemed an astonishing quantity of fish, and no day passed without hundreds of boxes being landed. I remembered a solitary fisherman on the Ross of Mull who used slug worm for fishing flounder in the Sound of Iona. He told me he had been getting good catches of small haddock in a bay on the north of the Ross. A trawler came in one night. 'After that I didn't see a tail.' He was not the sort of man who would exaggerate. He had no particular animus against the trawlers. He accepted them as he accepted bad weather. And he would have worked his fingers off rather than try for the dole.

A man in Tobermory visited forty creels one morning without getting a single lobster. He was very despondent and felt like throwing the whole business up. From Skye, round Ardnamurchan Point, and down the Sound of Mull, there was the same tale from the men with whom I talked. Somewhere thereabouts, I ran into the theory that trawling affected the lobster spawn. The trawlers can get blamed for too much – like giving a dog a bad name – and this theory sounded pretty far-fetched! Yet in the long run there is a balance in nature, so that, for example, one would not expect to find peregrine falcons where there was no other bird life. That trawlers poach inshore banks there can be no doubt. That the official effort to detect them is ludicrously inadequate there is likewise no doubt. One cannot blame the fishery cruiser, any more than one would blame a single gamekeeper for failing to keep down poaching in the whole of Argyll.

To blame the trawlers is to ask too much of human nature. Indeed, as I looked at these iron vessels, their rust whitened by salt water and gulls, I knew I was looking at the most daring vessels afloat, manned by the finest and most intrepid seamen to be found on any of the oceans of the world. They have the air of buccaneers. No slacking or grousing against the Government here. They take their living out of the teeth of danger, in the worst seas fought by man, and a slowly meandering fishery cruiser's gun or the wailing of a pack of crofters is not going to trouble them much. You won't stop trawling by appealing to something called a moral sense, certainly not in a world dominated by Stock Exchanges and by shore syndicates, which inform a skipper that his existence depends on getting boxes of fish. Besides, the power of these shore syndicates is felt in official places, in a way that the lack of power of the crofter-fisher is not.

The whole existing process is cumulative, and its end certain, so far as our old Highland life is concerned. That does not mean, of course, that the process could not be stopped or at least very tangibly affected. It could. Trawling could be stopped on the inshore banks tomorrow, for example, if the Government really wished to stop it; just as the Scottish herring fleet could be revitalised, if certain things happened to its organisation and the Government decided, for purposes of food and defence, that its seamen were too invaluable to lose. But we have discussed that before. Meantime, the one certain thing I have encountered in my cruise is the common decline of the West.

'But at least these trawlers bring a lot of business to Oban?'

He shook his head. 'They have the fish all ready in iced boxes, and load them direct on to the train for the south. That's all.'

We watched this neat dispatch of business. The train shunted on to the quay.

'Are there no local boats fishing from Oban?'

'There is supposed to be one,' he said.

And there we were back at a sore point. For there is something in the reputed lack of initiative of the West Coast man. How this has come about, by what discouragements and official repressions or neglect, by what succumbing to a feeling of hopelessness in the fight, it may not be easy to determine.

Then suddenly our thoughts got a queer twist. When the East Coast herring fishers – whose history proves them men of initiative, fearlessness, and a tremendous capacity for the most gruelling toil – are at last down and out, their boats derelict, under age and debt, will some chance visitor, eating trawl-caught fish from Hull in the hotels of Wick or Buckie, wonder at the supine local concerned no longer with catching fish but with wangling money out of the Buroo? Is that an impossible situation? In some degree, is it not happening already?

We could not find the solitary boat that was supposed to fish out of Oban, so we bought white fish in a shop and were assured that it was fresh and very good, as it had come direct from Aberdeen.

5

The Wonder Story of the Moray Firth

THERE WAS ONCE a TIME – AND old folk still alive can remember the tail-end of it – when the seaboard round the Moray Firth went up in a human blaze – as hectic a blaze as ever was seen in any gold rush to the Klondyke. In the whole history of the Highlands, I know nothing like it. And the story has always fascinated me because here, for once, Highlanders were suddenly given the chance to get gold, for themselves—and how they set about it! The Klondykers certainly had nothing on them. It threw – and, I maintain, still throws – a light on all those notions about Highlanders being indifferent or lazy. Give them the proper chance … however, let me stick to the story of what did happen when they got the chance.

The beginnings of the story coincide with the peak of the Clearances in these northern parts. From whole straths, up Kildonan way, the people were evicted and their homes destroyed. We all know something about that tragic business, and happily I am not concerned with it here. How reluctant we are even to remember it – and how pleasant to tell a story of another kind! If I mention it, then, it is because, though great numbers of the evicted were shipped to Canada, many of them built shacks by the seashore and managed to keep alive long enough to take part in the new great adventure – the adventure with the sea.

Behind them was the land – and they knew what had happened to them there. In front of them – the sea; and the wonderful thing about the sea was that it was free to them all. They could sink or swim in it. Haddock and cod and flukes and herring were not game within the meaning of any Act. What they could catch they could eat. Only, to begin with, they were not very good at the catching. Probably many of them, from far inland glens, had never even seen the sea, for pony tracks or drove roads were the means of communication then. However, they learned, and always there had been those, living near the coast, who had ventured out in a small boat from a wild creek or narrow beach. So knowledge spread and help was given in the way help always was given to neighbours in distress in any Highland community. To transgress the ancient law of hospitality brought deep shame.

Well, that was roughly the position along great stretches of the Moray Firth in the opening years of last century, and if, in what I am going to say, I stick in particular to the northern coast – from well south of Helmsdale right along to Wick – it is because here the difficulties were concentrated. In the first place, it had no hinterland with economic resources, no towns, no industries, no sources of capital for boats and gear; and, in the second place, from Helmsdale to Wick the coastline was – it still is – one menacing wall of cliff, with little more than stormy breaks in it, and few enough of them. To triumph, to make a Klondyke of the sea, *here*, must have seemed utterly unthinkable.

The position was even worse than that, for such historic efforts as had been made, by royal or parliamentary action, to encourage Scottish fisheries, had always, in the main, proved ineffective. Over a long period of time the Dutch had been the real sea-fishing masters, with their well-equipped fleets of boats and their accompanying large vessels or busses for curing herring at sea. The success of the Dutch is summed up in the old saying: 'Amsterdam was built on herring bones'.

Then someone had a thought, and the thought was a stroke of genius. More wonderful still, it was translated into an Act of Parliament, in the year 1809. And the stroke was this: that for every barrel of sound herring cured *on shore* a bounty would be paid of two shillings. Now there had long been a small bounty payment for fish *exported*. But here the bounty of two shillings was to be paid whether the barrel of herring was exported or not. No need now to emulate the Dutch way of catching and curing at sea. To the curer of one barrel of good herring *on shore*, a bounty of two shillings – or subsidy, as we would say.

That two shillings then were worth many times more than two shillings today does not give the whole picture, not for those folk whom I have mentioned, too many of them with miserable strips of land that in the best of seasons could hardly keep body and soul together. In the absence of written records, we have to use a little imagination, if we are going to get an echo of the kind of conversation that must have passed between them. And even then we would have to translate it from Gaelic, for Gaelic was the mother tongue from far south of Helmsdale to within a few miles of Wick – and, indeed, for another two generations. However, they came at the English in time and I can hear them sizing up the situation in 1809 like this: 'Boys, if we can get something that will float, and a herring net or two nets, and bring four or three creels of herring to the curer, we can be sure of two shillings in our hand, we can be sure of that whateverway – not to speak of what the curer will add to the two shillings, which should be another two shillings for us at the least, if there's competition among the curers at all. Four or maybe five shillings for a cran of herring – in our hand!' It was a big thought. And a thought they were free to multiply. The Highlander has never been deficient in imagination and he was a born hunter. The whole thing was right into his creel. It went to his head. And so he started.

Even the Government must have cheered, for in 1815 they lifted the two-shilling subsidy to four shillings. That did it! If the doing was necessary – but then the Government must have begun to realise that not only were these Highlanders hauling gold from the sea, but helping to sweep the Dutch off it. It had become a national affair in wealth – and international in trade and policy.

What extraordinary scenes must have been enacted then, scenes of contrivance and ingenuity, bargaining, a promise to pay the rare one who could lend a pound or two, a promise not in writing but, more solemnly, by a spit in the palm and a handshake!

By the courtesy of the Fishery Board – I suppose I should call it the Department of Agriculture and Fisheries now – I was given permission many years ago, when I was researching into this whole matter, to inspect official records where I could find them, and I can remember calling on the Fishery officer in Helmsdale and discovering a ledger of official transactions for that very year of 1815. At the moment I cannot recollect the exact number of curers already operating in Helmsdale in 1815, but if I say a round dozen I am near enough. There were entries also regarding fishing creeks from south of Helmsdale and north to Lybster, for Helmsdale then was the official headquarters of all that stretch of coast and its business centre. In this way I got a grasp of the earlier stages of this extraordinary story.

However, as we know only too well – stroke of genius or no stroke of genius – what the Government gives with one hand it has the other and stronger hand ever ready to take back. So in the 1820s the Government decreed that the subsidy would be withdrawn, not in one fell swoop, but shilling by shilling, until by 1830 the lot would be gone. You can imagine the outcry. Ruination! What happened was that the industry took the loss in its stride and swept on to greater triumphs. By the 1840s there were up to 250 boats fishing out of Helmsdale in the summer season. But the total of all the crews of the boats is only one item, for behind them were curers, coopers, women gutters and packers, makers of herring nets and creels, shop-keepers, carriers, seamen engaged in the export trade – a whole complex living swarm of human life. Then, remember that Helmsdale only started herring fishing less than 30 years before, in those years when the terrible Clearances were at their height.

I look at the map in my mind, with some of the fishing place-names south and north of Helmsdale: Embo, Golspie, Brora, Portgower, Helmsdale, Berriedale, Dunbeath. Latheronwheel, Forse, Swiney, Lybster. After that, Clyth and the high cliffs; with the remarkable Whaligoe, on the way to the great fishing port of Wick. Of course, Wick had long had commerce with the sea, but as late as 1767 its fishermen still regarded herring as bait for white fish. But by 1840 Wick had 428 native boats and 337 strange boats at the herring fishing. But again, by official record, *total* personnel engaged at the peak of the summer fishing was no less than 7,882. May I say, in passing, that anyone interested in such statistics, and in the kinds of boats and gear used, will find it all in that fascinating and authoritative book by Peter F Anson, called *Fishing Boats and Fisher Folk of the East Coast of Scotland*.

Meanwhile, let me glance at a more directly human aspect of the story and in a somewhat different light. In that same year, 1840, was published a Statistical Account of Scotland, written mostly by ministers of the Gospel about their various parishes. Here is the Reverend Charles Thomson counting the number of – no, not boats, but public houses in Wick and reaching a grand total of 45. Says he: 'The herring fishing has increased wealth, but also wickedness. No care is taken of the 10,000 young strangers of both sexes, crowded together with the inhabitants during the six weeks of the fishery and exposed to drink and every other temptation.' So he called the pubs, 'Seminaries of Satan and Belial'. Apparently on occasion up to 500 gallons of whisky were disposed of in a day in Wick. A fair dram, I admit! And how interesting it would be to find out just how and where and with what results that dram got drunk! But I have only time to balance this by another picture of life, from which Satan and Belial were certainly absent, and which continued to within living memory: that of the crews of hundreds upon hundreds of boats at sea on a quiet evening, after their nets had been shot, taking up, one after another, one of the Psalms of David, until it seemed the sea itself sang and the cliffs and the cottages were held in wonder.

A tireless, tough, and God-fearing people, taking their lives in their hands, on these treacherous coasts, in their small open boats – and sending their tens of thousands of barrels of herring deep into Germany, into the Baltic Sea, and far into Russia.

I cannot pursue the story here and tell how boats got bigger, got decked, until finally the steam drifter took over and concentrated the herring fishing in a few large ports. Many of the smaller creeks, which once knew such a surge of warm life, are now quite derelict. But the men and women of that time – for nearly a whole century – did something more remarkable, with more wonder of achievement in it, than any story of mine could ever adequately tell.

6

The French Smack

LESS THAN TWO MONTHS BEFORE the outbreak of war I was on an island in the Outer Hebrides, the guest of a seaman who had a thirty-five-foot fishing boat driven by an old Kelvin engine. I have described elsewhere how we loaded her with young sheep and set out for certain distant rock-islands in the Atlantic, whose green tops were used as grazing grounds. I did little more than mention a French smack encountered in that wild remote region, because our real interest centred in the exciting business of pushing the sheep we had taken with us up the cliffs and, even more difficult, driving those on top down and into the heaving boat. Many an actor has gained distinction on the films for less hazardous work than that accomplished by two or three young members of our crew on these rock-faces.

Events have happened since then, however, to bring the French smack into memory's picture with particular vividness. She was first sighted when the skipper and I were down below, and by the time we got on deck, she was disappearing round one of the high islands. I gathered from the remarks that were passed that she was a Frenchman and that she was poaching. Poaching what? Lobsters. And at that I was assailed by a shock of wonder and admiration. I knew of the grumblings and lassitude of some of our native lobster-fishers – and on that heaving sea it seemed a far cry to France!

However, when we had finished with two of the islets, and were rounding some rocks to deal with two more, we came upon the Frenchman innocently at anchor, and I thought to myself that the skipper had been mistaken. How could they be sure that this vessel was engaged on such an enterprise so far from her own shores? The answer came with dramatic swiftness. There was a yell from the look-out, the wheel was spun, and I just had time to see some cork floats being sucked under before the engine gave a mighty thump – and then silence. The engineer's astonished head appeared. The gear lever had all but hit him. For one moment he had thought the whole engine was being torn out of the boat. We had fouled the rope of presumably one of the Frenchman's lobster pots in the open seaway!

It was surely a moment that warranted on the part of our quiet-mannered skipper a slight exclamation of annoyance, to put it mildly. There was none. It was now after ten o'clock at night and the overcast sky, if not immediately threatening, did not herald serene weather. There was no harbour here, no place where a boat could be beached; nothing but rock walls and, in one or two spots, the most fugitive of anchorages. I remembered the trouble my wife and I had had when the painter of our dinghy had been sucked down by the shaft and wound round it so tightly that after we had cut the rope we could not disengage the coils from the shaft, and could not shove the gear-lever forward or astern.

When at last the rope had been cut on both sides of the shaft, I saw the skipper quietly taking the severed floats on board. After one of the lads had worked for a time at the coils round the shaft with the boathook, it was decided to try the engine. She started; she took the gear lever; she went forward. At twenty-five years a Kelvin can be moody, as I knew; but – 'Mohooker, she's tough!'

We slid on, heading for our landing, and passed close by the Frenchman. 'Has anyone a pencil?' There was a hunt, and finally her name and registry number were duly noted.

But meantime not a sign from the Frenchman. Not a light. It might have been a ship of the dead. A deserted pirate ship. Her mainsail, all set, clacked loudly as it swung from side to side in the wind, while she rolled in the swell. Green-painted, with square stern, she was not a big vessel. I doubted if she was more than forty-five feet. She was beamy certainly, but when I was told that in addition to all her gear of ropes and lobster pots, she carried a great internal tank in which she stored alive a vast catch of lobsters, I was inclined to be sceptical. But I was wrong. Why? Because a vessel like her had been caught by the Fishery Cruiser and all her gear and lobsters confiscated and duly sold at public auction. Where? In Stornoway. There had been well over a thousand fathom of new rope; and who should know better than our skipper who had bought a large part of it? Which was that!

And the lobsters?

No one wanted to buy them, until one man thought he would have a long shot, if he got them cheap. One of the crew alleged that the purchaser netted about a thousand pounds for the lot. But that seemed fantastic, for a simple sum in arithmetic made the total of lobsters too colossal surely for so small a vessel to carry.

'I'm not so sure,' said our master. 'What the skipper himself said was that if he had got off with it, it would have been worth to him a small fortune."

'Would he have made direct for a port in France and sold them there?'

'I don't think so, I believe they sail up the Mediterranean and sell them at a good price from place to place.'

I looked at the Frenchman again and, inwardly, saluted him. I thought of the Frenchmen from the little ports of Brittany who engage in the Iceland fishings. Great seamen!

'Whenever we get back, we'll let the Fishery Cruiser know.' There is a duty one owes to the fishing interests of one's own people.

I asked what evidence had we, after all, that the Frenchman had set the pots? It couldn't be said that he was sheltering here from bad weather, perhaps, but still if, on a voyage, he found himself running out of fresh meat and supposing – supposing he alleged that he had come in to make the hunt on certain wild goat-like sheep that inhabited these rocks?

The skipper smiled. The evidence would be all right.

If she comes in time I thought to myself; for I had a notion that though there were no visible heads on the *Marie Louise,* there were many invisible eyes.

The Frenchman was forgotten in the incidents of the hours that followed, and one that gave me a real fright is still clearly etched. I was going down some steps in the rock, shepherding the rear, when directly beneath I suddenly saw a figure between me and the sea. I knew at once what had happened. A sheep had left the lighthouse steps where, between them and the brink of the cliff, was a yard or so of irregular rock. One of our lads had followed and, as I looked, I saw his body stand out from the rock clearly defined against the white surf far below. As his body swayed, wrestling with the sheep, I thought he was gone. It was not a pleasant moment.

But we got our job finished, and about one o'clock in the morning, in that dim half-light of the summer night that never grows dark in these regions, we cried farewell to the men of the lighthouse and turned to the sea – and proved there was life in the pirate ship after all, for now at her masthead, like a large French glow worm, shone her riding-light! She had seen us all right – if she had never let on! There was a smile all round at that. The yard-arm still clacked as she heaved at anchor. We nosed past her with a wary eye for lobster entanglements.

There was an incident on that homeward trip that may be worth noting, before I mention how I ran into Kenneth on the quays of Stornoway some days later and got my last news of the Frenchman.

When we had left the heavy roll of the Western Ocean behind and come into sheltered waterways between small islands, the morning was well advanced, but there was still no human life about the cottages seen here and there beyond sandy shores or in little bights of the land. They have their own conception of time in the West and early-rising is not greatly favoured. The cottages were still asleep and there was peace everywhere. Though in truth it did not seem sleep so much as an arrestment of time in a clear enchanted air. As we had now been on our feet and tossing about or climbing for some twenty-four hours, I had a rather pleasant bodiless feeling myself. It is a feeling that one may have to go through considerable stress to attain, but it does bring with it a certain serenity, a smoothing away of all ill-humours, a sense of companionship, a clear apprehension of the friendliness of peace and of the idiocy of strife. Indeed in such a moment the conception of brutal strife belongs to another order of existence; it does not seem evil so much as remote and senseless and idiotic. In that moment, too, is born the positive conception that, quite simply, life is good, that it is a rare and lovely thing in its own right, like the blooming of a wild rose. And also in that moment sleep, death itself, is apprehended in the clear air of the mind as a 'translation'; translation into what, one does not know, except that it holds in these fleeting instants a mystery one no longer fears.

But mechanism put an end to all speculation when the engine suddenly conked out. The paraffin tanks were dry!

What should we do? We had a long way to go yet. Try to sail her in the slight wind? Or use our only remaining fuel, the tin of petrol, required for starting her? Many factors were involved. The second and last trip was to take place immediately, while the weather held. The skipper had a good stock of paraffin at home, but no petrol, which had to be brought from Stornoway. If he used all his supply of petrol now? And, in any case, there was hardly enough to take us to the ferry, and we had a long way to go beyond that before we could land our sheep. There was a thought – the ferry! Who knew but that petrol and paraffin, belonging to some one or other, might not be sitting in large tins on the jetty? To me it seemed fabulously unlikely, but still it could not be ruled out categorically as impossible! And, anyway, why meet trouble until it met us?

'I think you may as well put the petrol in her.'

'Very good,' and in a short time we were under way. We pressed up the sound, and on the last little wash of petrol in the tank, we drew alongside the small and utterly deserted jetty.

Obviously no life had stirred there this morning. But our eyes were arrested by two interesting looking drums. We landed and tapped them. They were full. We unscrewed the bungs. There was petrol in one drum and paraffin in the other! And they were completely innocent of any label of ownership.

'Isn't that luck?' said Kenneth calmly, going down for empty petrol tins. I looked at the skipper in, I suppose, a wordless way.

'The owner will know,' he said, 'that the one who took it needed it. That's the way we work here. Besides, I'm fairly sure I know whose it is.' He noted the quantities withdrawn from the drums, so that they could be made good in due course.

It was not the sort of happening designed to lessen an early-morning faith in either the goodness of life or its magic! I could not take part in the second trip into the Atlantic but, as I said, I ran into Kenneth on the quays of Stornoway some days later and would have passed him by had he not hailed me, for he was all dressed up in his naval suiting.

'Where away?' I asked in astonishment.

As a Naval Reserve he had been suddenly called up and was on his way south to join the fleet. 'For a couple of months,' he added. 'I don't think there will be any trouble.'

'I don't think so,' I agreed.

War seemed too impossible a madness on that July morning.

Off and on, the Frenchman had been in my mind, and now I asked for the latest news of him. Kenneth smiled. The Fishery Cruiser, it appeared, had gone out that way – to find the Frenchman gone. 'Not a sign of him!' We laughed.

'Ah, well,' said Kenneth, 'I would have been sorry if anything had happened. It was plucky of them coming all that way.'

We agreed heartily, and when we shook hands I promised to come out to see them all soon again.

It may not be soon now, but I hope that it will be again, and that I shall see them all. One conviction remains, that there is nothing above the sea or on the sea or under the sea can stop, in their natural alliance, those lads I knew and the daring seamen of the *Marie Louise.*

7

The First Salmon

U<small>P IN THE DARK OF</small> a February morning, with a good three hours' motoring in front of us before we reach the river. No salmon has yet been grassed, although the opening day is already a fortnight old. Perhaps we shall be lucky enough to land the first for the season! Worth a smile; but then I have heard many an owner of a half-ticket in the Irish Sweep (before the legal ban, of course) confidently dispose of a fortune before the drum had spoken.

It was a good morning to jet about it anyway, and when we came to the top of the southern escarpment that overlooks the Dornoch Firth and beheld the panorama in front of us – surely the most magnificent on the whole East Coast – our hopes were even heightened, despite the long white streamers on the water that told so frankly the strength of the wind. There and then we modestly decided that we should get only one fish, and as my friend, though a sound angler, had never previously thrown a salmon fly, we agreed that he was bound to be the lucky one. I always think it is wise to be clear on these matters beforehand. A certain small amount of excitement, of course, would come my way, but it would take the shape of kelt.

'Will you know it's a kelt whenever you hook it?' asked my friend.

'At once,' I replied, almost sadly, visualising the lazy turn-over of the body under the water, the wallop on the surface, the eel-like wriggle, the sluggishness, the lack of power and fire.

But on a morning like this, driving along that ever-varying north-east coast, with its mountain curves and pines, its bronze bracken and brown birch woods, its ravines and bridges over little streams, what would it matter whether one had luck or not? (Which merely made the luck seem all the more certain!) The engine of the car sang away to itself. And even the miles of 'Road under Repair' (why should this form of desolation always stretch for about ten miles?) merely made us change the nature of our language, not its positive tone.

There may be better places to arrive at than the cosy private parlour or office of an hotel, but if so I have been unlucky. And while we were having what we had, the talk got going and a gillie was persuaded to tell his famous story of the man who went to bury his third wife. By the time we got to the river we were in good trim.

And the river was in good trim, too – except for the wind, which blew so strongly upstream that my fourteen-foot rod was voted too light and our host presented me with his own, which was sixteen feet (if it wasn't eighteen) and carried a fly fully as long as a man's middle finger. 'It is guaranteed,' he said in his pleasant way, 'to break your back inside two hours. After that you will be sore for three days.' Which would have been all that one might desire – were it not for the contrary wind that required at least a double expenditure of force.

Down through some bushes and over grey grass and yellow moss, and there was the first pool, dark moving water with white flecks and ripples. How lovely a thing a fishing pool is! It has intimacy and ancestry in it. Old as the blood-stream itself, and as full of intimations and hopes and queer elusive memories. There is an urgency to be at it, and a contrary impulse to take one's time, to do things leisurely and rightly, with a glance up the glen and a glance down, smiling at the flow of the hills or at oneself. The world can get on with its rearmament now, or with any other perverse or bloody madness! All through the dark winter months, the universal cry has been: 'The world needs peace.' Standing by the river's brim, one wonders if it is merely the soul of a man, this man and that man, that needs peace. Peace like this, immemorial and good, lapping against the flesh, soaking into the bone and to the marrow of the bone. Peace not as an absence of war, but peace as a living reality, a positive thing like the scent of the bushes and the ling, or the first notes of a young chaffinch, or the cry of a newly arrived peewit – or the song of the reel.

How carefully one fishes the first pool! And reflects at the end of it that it would be wrong to get anything in the first pool. Nothing worth doing should be easy. One salmon a day should satisfy any man. And it should be caught at some moment when he would almost have been justified in being careless – but wasn't. Yet truth compels me to say that I once caught an eighteen-pounder in my second full cast, that I have never forgotten it, and that I am dogged by an unworthy desire to find out again precisely how it felt.

There was to be no eighteen-pounder this day. And by the time I had finished the pool, the vertebral bones were creaking, certain muscles were tremulous, and the wind performed its only useful service by drying a bared forehead. Hitherto I had thought the wind rather cold, but now as I sat down to change my fly, I realised that it was a spring wind full of promise of long days to come. The year was opening its slow door to summer pastures. There is an emotion of gratitude to this old scarred earth that runs very deep. Or is it very high, like blown thistledown in a sunny wind? About as light as that, anyhow, and with an echo of laughter blown with it.

And so to the next pool. And to the next. With never a tug or a swirl or a rise anywhere. No, the salmon cannot have started running yet. In the last few years, I was told, the salmon in this river have decidedly been running later – to the extent even of affecting the letting. No reason could be given for this. And the whim might pass.

'Have you no special theory?' I asked my host, making my last cast at the tail of the pool and half turning my head. But I never got the answer, for in the same instant I was 'in him'.

A kelt? No, said my host. No, said the gillie. Decidedly no, thought I, as he took the current with a strong head. There had been no turn-over, with the silver gleaming ruddy through the brown water – a thing one should not see until the fight is ending. After five minutes I would have offered fantastic odds that I was in a clean fish, had there been anyone to take me. Indeed I had landed many clean fish that had behaved with even slower stubbornness. I could not get him to show himself. And when at last he was tiring, I began to grow anxious. My host was ready with the gaff. The gillie was all eyes. I brought him in. He showed himself. It was a kelt – foul-hooked!

The gillie tailed him, undid the hook, and he sailed away into deep water, none the worse.

The first part of my prophecy had come true.

43

And the second part followed in due course, for my friend got into a salmon. Again speculation was favourable – but this time with the mighty difference that it was correct. A clean-run hen fish of seven pounds, exquisite in line as anything that was ever created. The first fish of the season, of the year. The river was at last open.

It was an occasion to be toasted properly, with bonnets off. Even to be toasted twice. Nature was fulfilling her ancient contract to man. The local reporter could put his paragraph in the press.

We got no more fish that day. Which was right and proper. We had started in the half-light of the morning, full of hope. We left in the half-light of the evening, full of blessed tiredness and hospitality, convinced that fine men lived in a fine world – whose life-streams are its rivers.

8

Black Cattle in Lochaber

WHAT SORT OF BEASTS WERE the 'black cattle' of the Highlands? In many places and of old men I had asked the question but never could get a definite answer. Yet obviously if I was to draw a clear picture of the old Highland economy, of which black cattle and sheep were the mainstay, the inner eye must first be able to see the real animals roaming over outfield and hill-pasture. There would be a difference, for example, in the human reaction to a douce black-polled cow as compared with that to a dun-haired, long-horned Highland cow, and if the reaction was not visible but of the stuff of the imagination or the unconscious it might be none the less important on that account. In truth, it was just as necessary for me to know the kind of cow as the kind of scenery. Smooth low-land country has a quite different effect on the mind from that of mountains and glens.

But how difficult, often, to get exact information about what were the affairs or objects of everyday! Except for two or three travellers' books, what would we know about the past domestic and cultural life of the Highlands? I got my description of the black cattle in the notes to a poem, called 'The Grampians Desolate', by Alexander Campbell, published in 1804. Here it is: 'A cow, of the Sky or Kintail breed, is a remarkably handsome animal; it carries its head erect, which gives it a deer-like air, peculiar to the cattle of those districts. Besides a straight, thick back, deep in the rib, elevated head and neck; small blue or clear yellow horns, tipt with black, and sharp-pointed; the hide of a dark brown colour,

45

short legs, and large bushy tail – are marks truly characteristic of a cow, ox, or bull, of the real highland breed of black-cattle.'

The other month I saw a beast approximating very closely to this description, and what specially caught my eye was the strength and fulness of the shoulders and neck. The head was up like a stag's and the brute looked as if it could charge. It was well knit, full of vitality, and native to its rough heathery background. It seemed much hardier than those very picturesque 'Highland cattle' we see now and then at cattle sales or on picture postcards, though clearly of the same breed.

The notes to the poem fill half the book and they are often fascinating. The verses themselves 'are professedly', says the author, 'of a political cast; but, disclaiming all connection with the politics of the day, they aim at something very different – and that is, to call the attention of good men, wherever dispersed throughout our island, to the manifold and great evils arising from the introduction of that system which has within these last forty years spread among the Grampians and Western Isles, and is the leading cause of a Depopulation that threatens to extirpate the ancient race of inhabitants of those districts'. The system, of course, was that of sheep farms – or sheep-stores, as they were called.

The author gives details of the earliest beginnings of the system, and what he has to say on the old economy which sheep-farming supplanted is of particular interest to those of us who today would like to see the Highlands coming into their human own once more.

As for the black cattle, so he has a good word for the native sheep, which Donald Monro mentions to have seen 'feeding masterless, partayning peculiarly to no man', about the end of the fifteenth century.

Of the Linton or black-faced sheep which were introduced to the Highlands, he writes: 'Without doubt, the Linton sheep are hardy, and easily reared in mountainous districts; but then they are very subject to a loathsome and fatal distemper called braxy, which carries off prodigious numbers … But the native breed seem not liable to that disease, as, previous to the introduction of the Linton breed, I am credibly informed no such disorder as *braxy* was ever heard of in the Grampians or Western Isles.' He then contrasts the `shaggy coarse' wool of the black-face with the native fleeces `of a texture remarkable for fineness, closeness, and softness to the sense of touch; and when sent to the market fetch double, nay, treble the sum the merchant allows for the coarse wool'. And the flesh of the black-face, however preferable to that of the Leicester, is still 'infinitely inferior to the small, delicious mutton of the real native breed'.

And the author knows at first hand what he is talking about, for he took in hand the management of the family affairs in Lochaber when his son-in-law, Captain Alexander McDonell, was serving abroad with his regiment (1791 to 1799); 'a pretty considerable live-stock concern, consisting mostly of sheep and black cattle, which were kept on the upland pastures on the side of Lochtraig, a part of the extensive Highland property of his grace the Duke of Gordon in the district of the Grampians'. On the low ground were various farms carrying a considerable number of sub-tenants. These were what we would call crofting areas, and the author says that the mode of their farming 'was wretched in the extreme'. Clearly, though his sympathies were with them as children of the Gael, he considered them a somewhat thriftless and lazy lot. They built their houses of turf, 'usually cut from the best sward of the whole farm, being the firmest, consequently the best, for that purpose'. They did not trouble to collect manure, and when any was needed for potatoes or barley, down they hauled the end of the house which had been well smoked, 'and being ready to crumble to pieces, it was most excellent manure'. Then they cut more sward and re-built!

When the author took charge in 1794 he decided to put an end to this. Besides, to see the women working hard while their men idled about was a bit too much. Not, as he points out, that the women objected. They worked 'cheerfully, for they always alleged that too severe labour did much harm to the make, vigour and constitution of their lords and masters, and consequently spoiled the breed'. Moreover, when they did work, the men kept their plaids on. Clearly a difficult matter for the author to regard with equanimity.

But what to do about it? Now the author had a manager, a wily and able man named Macnab, and his solution was simple: Put up the rents, said Macnab, and that will quicken 'the exertions of individuals who otherwise were rather less inclined to industry, when they found both ends meet (as the saying is) and slip easily through life'.

'What sir!' exclaimed our author, 'ruin our tenants by a *rack-rent!* – are you in your sober senses?'

'Perfectly so,' replied Macnab.

And the scheme was put 'to the test of experiment in the year 1796. And in

1797 a farther rise was exacted, at which they murmured much, and threatened to leave their possessions in disgust.' But the author was the less alarmed because the price of cattle was on the rise as a result of war, and he had already found that the use of the word *ejection* would achieve almost anything, including the removal of the plaids during toil.

But our author was not satisfied. He was a man of considerable foresight and decided that what was really needed in these crofting areas was joint-stock farming, a co-operative combine. This, he was satisfied, would at one and the same time increase the size of the rent-roll and better the conditions of the tenants. So he set about it in one area, and in the end 'prodigious opposition and cabal were at length subdued'.

The experiment proved financially successful for all concerned. 'Still, however, they did not relish the change of system; and the rest of their neighbours, who had not yet submitted to this mode of uniformity of goods and gear, agreeable to rural economy, sneered at their simplicity – they also were invited in turn to unite in the community of the joint-stock system, but they flew one and all in the face of it, and gave it a most firm and decided opposition.'

And now for the first time the magic word ejection refused to work. The author was 'inwardly troubled'. But by this time he had not only tasted the dictator's power, but realised what is the mainspring of the dictator's philosophy. Though inwardly troubled, he decided that 'what is once begun, when substantially good, ought steadily to be persisted in; and I had resolved – it must, and shall be done – and it was done'.

At the end of all protestations the threat of ejection worked.

And the new system also worked apparently, for the author 'cannot help recommending it to the consideration of reputable tacksmen, thoughtful land-holders, and patriotic members of the British Senate, as it appears to me, from the trial made previous to the year 1799, and since that period, under circumstances, too, verging toward the oppressive system of rack-rent – that the population and means of subsistence in the very wilderness of Lochaber, do actually exist, and may still be preserved by wise, and prudent management.'

This was an extremely interesting conclusion to have been reached through the joint-stock experiment. And indeed in recent years we have seen something of the kind work satisfactorily in our club sheep-farms in the Highlands, particularly when they were set up under favourable financial conditions (which was not always the case). Also there is raised the important consideration of sheep and native cattle. Anyway, here was an enlightened landlord, quite aware of the evils of rack-rents, turning the wilderness of Lochaber into a going concern for the human inhabitants, the black cattle, and the native sheep. That he was humane and scholarly, with a true aptitude for the customs and culture of the folk, is abundantly clear.

But now his drama takes a new and revealing turn. His son-in-law obtained leave of absence from his regiment, then in Portugal, and our author placed before him, on his return home, the joint-stock scheme which he had brought into being.

Captain McDonell was perfectly satisfied. It happened, however, that his lease from the Duke of Gordon was about to expire, so 'he wrote to his Grace, reminding him of old times; (for the Keappoch family were vassals of the family of Gordon for many centuries), and requesting a renewal of his lease, but without putting Keappoch on the same footing as the general run of tacksmen in that part of the country. His Grace was pleased to answer Captain McDonell's letter in the handsomest manner; and in one paragraph expresses himself thus: "I continue disposed to mark my regard for your family, by a degree of favour which no common tenant could expect."'

Meantime the prosperous conditions of the joint-stock lands had been 'marked by the neighbouring tacksmen and shepherds with an evil eye'. There was a boom in the new sheep-farms that swept the tenants off the land. The clearances were coming into full swing. And then follows this delicate exercise in irony by our author: 'Secret offers were given in, amounting to four times the former rent of my friend's possessions; but the noble proprietor, true to his promise, with a princely munificence, says in his second letter, dated London, May 15th, 1799, which now lies before me, that he might let the possessions for four times the former rent, but that he did not mean to put him on the footing of ordinary tenants; and therefore he was willing to let him continue to hold the possessions for one-fourth less than what was actually offered'.

In short, Keappoch's rent was trebled at one stroke by his gracious overlord!

Keappoch, we are informed, was 'amazed at the prodigious rise', and did not know what to do, for he had merely been defending his country abroad for seven years 'during the hottest of the war'.

As things were, he could not pay the rent demanded. Clear the folk off the land? Turn the whole into a sheep-run? But his family interest was at stake. What to do?

And our author comes to his aid thus: 'Apprize the tenants … you are their chieftain; some of them fought by the side of your grandfather Keappoch who fell on Culloden-moor; and several of them fought with your father on that day when our immortal Wolfe fell on the plains of Quebec – try what they will do of their own accord … leave the affair to their own management, and wait patiently the event.'

So Captain McDonell laid the matter before them, and the third turn to the drama came in their unanimous resolve 'That they would support their chieftain to the last shilling.'

And this they did, paying 'punctually their proportion of rent, notwithstanding its absolutely verging on that hateful and alarming evil, rack-rent'.

All of which was perhaps hardly a drama, little more than a curtain-raiser, a prelude, to the ferocity with which the magic word ejection then set about clearing the glens and the straths of the Highlands. But it has its moments of illumination in matters, both empirical and imperial.

9

On Backgrounds

I HAVE BEEN READING SOME long-short stories by Somerset Maugham with re-newed admiration for his technique, his wit, and his detached and some-times profound understanding of human motive. But what has struck me more than ever before is how essentially English this writer is. His theme more often than not is cast in the ends of the earth, in Samoa, in Borneo, on the Siberian railway. Down a side street in Singapore, he will introduce us to a house where the daugh-ters of joy are all Japanese, or all Chinese, with the perfect discretion, the tolerant human sympathy of the man of the world, but always the man of the world who is also the civilised Englishman. The painted faces of the Chinese girls 'were like masks. They looked at the stranger with black derisive eyes. They were strangely inhuman.' For the purpose of this story nothing could be more complete than that swift, sure note.

Across eastern seas, in strange estuaries, with the lonely white man or two white men of the outpost, in virgin forest – everywhere the eyes look and see and pass on, with that same penetration and that same calm restlessness. For it is not an obvious restlessness of the spirit seeking satisfaction, never a disturbing intrusion of the ego or soul seeking fulfilment, but always a continuous curiosity that observes in passing because, after all, there is little more to be done, and certainly nothing more by the artist. To expect any-thing other than the chance happening, the momentary drama, and the evanescent pattern that happening and drama describe, is to ask of life what detached observation is unable to find in it. In any case, here are the findings, here are the stories, and if you are interested in the didactic processes of judgement, well, that is your personal affair. You may permit yourself the naive pleasure of imagining on the part of the author a faint shrug, a sardonic expression this side of a smile, but no more, or you would become talkative and ingenuous, while if you took a few steps beyond, you would be – Mr. Maugham often uses the word – flamboyant. Indeed you might then be on the verge of becoming interesting. But still, you would be flamboyant. And things often happen to the flamboyant of a dreadful nature. You might find yourself half in and half out the water on a South Sea beach with your throat cut, or lost in a primeval jungle whose green descends like a merciful curtain to hide the horrors of your unimaginable death.

But to appreciate how extremely well-bred is this art, you have to read Mr. Maugham when he is dealing with English upper-class life, with someone's place in the country or with that attractive mixture of social privilege and highbrow unconventionality that appears to be London's special distinction. Now he is at home, where he belongs, and to point contrast, he introduces his cosmopolitan element, say his Jew. We see the Jew of the third generation of ownership of a large, perfectly run English estate trying to be the English gentleman. Here Mr. Maugham's insight is infallible and its expression flawless. Irony supervenes, but it is an irony of understanding, especially understanding of the Jew who, in the third generation, by the occult impulse of blood or race, prefers piano-playing to a title and an English estate, who would ultimately rather be a Jew of the ghetto than an English gentleman. In the climax the Jew does not even blow out his brains; he puts his sporting gun to his breast and blows out his heart. So far as Mr. Maugham's irony may ever be considered partial, it may here be seen directed against the conception of the English gentleman, a conception static in its behaviour pattern, repressive of impulse, of art, lest its supreme ruling power be endangered. Almost, indeed, it seems that this repressive power is too much for so sensitive an artist and thus gets him wandering about the ends of the earth.

But however that may be – and no man can know all the factors behind his simplest motive – at least here we see an effort at the creation of a cosmopolitan understanding, a cosmopolitan art. Nothing could be further removed from the provincial in subject matter and style than Mr. Maugham's writings. Yet no writing with which I am acquainted is so surely English in manner and essence. It may even be the English of a certain social class, the expression of its particular culture, but it is palpably there, and nowhere does one become more conscious of it than down, say, a side street in Singapore.

There is no intention here to assess the value of this well-known writer's work. In these pages now and again I have tried to estimate the value and meaning of tradition. I think it is important that in Scotland, whose traditions have been weakening over a long period, we should get some sort of notion of what tradition means, particularly as we hear so much these days of universal brotherhood and the evils of nationalism, for nothing is so destructive of any kind of standards, whether of behaviour or of art, than just such vague hearsay or uplift.

Now, it may appear that I have been concerned to show that here we have a highly cultured writer who is a product of his background, who cannot get away from this background, and who to that extent is handicapped in his effort to achieve a universal art. Than this conclusion nothing could be further from the truth. It is his background, its very limitations, its discipline, that has helped him to achieve what he has achieved. All art is a matter of selection, and selection means limitations and discipline. You cannot draw without a pencil, nor write without a pen, nor type without the irreducible mechanism of a typewriter. You are limited by the size of your canvas, by the conventions of your medium in paint or word. Mind and instinct have been conditioned and shaped by background (which includes tradition), have been given by it standards of judgement, often unconscious, subtle, and exhibited in reaction as well as action. We rely on such standards at critical moments. They are our strength, not our weakness. Their limitation is something we can grip and lean against or use like a tool or a weapon. They are in any case the only real things at hand. One cannot lean against vague uplift. At the critical moment it isn't there, and a man lands on his back to perceive, with some dismay, his heels where his head should be.

How great the individual achievement may be is another matter – is, in fact, an individual affair. Unless a man be potentially great in himself he cannot achieve greatness. But what concerns us here is that a living tradition is an aid to achievement, and the lack of it a deterrent. So simple a statement may admit of some qualification, but essentially it is true. One may say, for example, with his publishers, that Maugham is distinguished by 'his almost surgical dissection of human nature'. Many certainly find him lacking in warmth, and some are conscious not merely of a penetrating sardonic intelligence that is not greatly impressed by the spectacle of life but also of a pervasive something that affects them like the thought of cruelty. But if we revert to the conception of the English gentleman, with its static behaviour pattern, its innate desire for continued dominance, and therefore its necessary antipathy to art (which is forever working a revolution in mental attitude), we can at least imagine, in Mr. Maugham's case, his need for dealing with it in no less drastic a manner than by a surgical dissection. If we go the length of saying that the static conception has frustrated the artist, then even a pervasive air of something approaching the thought of cruelty in his reaction, however unconscious, is not inconceivable. In any case, all such qualification or discussion does not take the writer away from his background; on the contrary, it draws him ever nearer to its core.

But it is impossible to deal here with this matter at any length, although a 'surgical dissection' along the lines suggested might produce some interesting results, particularly when we got the length of the ultimate English Empire ruler over against the ultimate English artist. There may be some-thing more significant in all this than is usually contemplated by the normal processes of literary criticism. Perhaps that is why it is so difficult for his contemporaries, even for the artist himself, to realise wherein his unique significance lies.

Meantime, however, our concern in these pages is not with the English tradition but with our own. If we can illustrate our subject from outside, that is all to the good. One may now be struck by that note on the Chinese girls and wonder, with not unpleasant speculation, what was the nature of the derision in the 'derisive eyes' and why, being delightfully human, they were yet 'strangely inhuman'.

Not a long time ago, I tuned in to one of those ceilidh broadcasts from a certain Highland locality and could readily imagine the impression created on musical ears listening in alien detachment. The voices were poor, the singing of doubtful merit, and the whole affair might well seem artificial, trumped up, and altogether a rather miserable show. It was so easy to imagine, in contrast, the slickness of an English comedy production, or the perfect unison of Welsh singing, its force and finish. Why should that be so? What has happened to tradition here? And, in particular, what does really take place inside the ceilidh, and how is a certain curious quality of folk intimacy affected by translation into a public performance?

All this is more than a problem in literary values. It is finally a problem in life values. We get the greatest satisfaction out of life when our back-ground is peopled by those to whom we are akin and who enjoy a tradition that is alive and dynamic. A distinguished anthropologist, touching on the 'gregarious impulse', quotes with approval from McDougal's *Introduction to Social Psychology:* 'In any human being the instinct operates most powerfully in relation to, and receives the highest degree of satisfaction from the presence of, the human beings who most closely resemble that individual, those who behave in like manner and respond to the same situations with similar emotions.'

In recent years the field anthropologist has done a lot to help us realise how much we are the children of our background, of our own particular culture pattern, however fondly we may have believed that ours was the only 'right' and therefore universally applicable one.

10
On Tradition

AT THE MERE MENTION OF the word 'tradition' some of us grow impatient, feeling that we have had too much of the stuff, that the world at the moment is all too literally and painfully sick of its effects, and that until we sweep its encumbering mess into limbo we shall have no new brave world.

There is something invigorating and hopeful in the thought of a clean sweep and a fresh start. Privilege, religious persecution, old school ties, economic injustice, systematic brutality, social taboos, misunderstood sex – let us put a depth charge under the lot and leave the wreckage to the black bottom of the Atlantic. Nor is this always a vague attitude – as we soon find out if we make even a cursory study of what is called advanced thought in specific fields of human endeavour, such as, say, politics and literature. In politics we talk of the revolutionary principle. Not gradualism, not a slow evolutionary process, but revolution, the clean sweep and a quite new beginning. In one very advanced literary periodical, formerly published in Paris, certain words, such as beauty, were taboo. I remember a poem in it to the effect that if a person mentioned the word 'beauty', the poet would reply with a very rude word indeed, and if the person persisted in mentioning the word 'beauty', the poet would leave the room on the principle that sexual advances were being made to him.

Now all this is interesting and significant, and if the clean sweep could be made and we could start off fresh and healthy, amid social equality and with new conceptions of (not to mention the thrill of a new word for) beauty, then surely all of us would plump for the depth charge. But alas! this whole attitude would appear to arise from wishful thinking. Not that one need object to wishful thinking, for at least it can be less harmful than some other kinds of thinking, but it does tend to forget basic facts, and the trouble with basic facts is just that they will not be ignored indefinitely. That may be a pity because their irruption can be a nuisance, and sometimes a calamity, and often, in truth, we feel we could get on very well without being reminded of them at all.

Even my newspaper, however, persists in reminding me of them. Here is a paragraph explaining how some of our gallant airmen who have crashed are being successfully treated for shock. Now the treatment does not consist in dealing with the fear, the noise, the shock of the actual terrifying experience itself. It consists in going back into the childhood of the airman and finding an incident there which he has completely forgotten and which, indeed, requires some considerable effort on the part of his doctor to bring up into his conscious mind. When this long-forgotten experience, this little basic fact lurking in the black deeps, is brought to the surface and looked at and understood, then at last the victim of shock finds relief and goes onward again.

In short, it seems that we cannot get entirely away from our past, that we cannot blow up tradition, for our roots are there, however deep and how-ever dark. But the psychologist has shown us this singular fact, namely, that to attempt to cover up or sink deep some ill or evil in our past may be worse than futile. What, in the hour of our trial, we have got to do, on the contrary, is to fish it up, to examine it, to understand it, and, in understanding, to be freed from its hidden compulsion. If this is true for medical science in the case of the individual, the chances are that it is true for political science in the case of nations, which are aggregates of individuals. Accordingly, if war is in fact an evil that resides in nationality, we can hardly hope to get rid of this evil by the revolutionary process of denying nationality and aspiring to a nationless world. As we have seen, we can deny basic facts only at our peril, and nations are at the moment very basic facts indeed. Only when each nation sees the war evil within itself, sees it, understands it, and overcomes it, will the next step towards international harmony inevitably rise.

Unfortunately this business of analysis is often difficult and irksome. Even the person who gives himself up to be psycho-analysed for his own good, can become so appalled at the nature of what lies hidden in him that he may resort to all sorts of dodges to hang on to his old respectable image of himself. And such an individual is not blatant, in the way a nation almost invariably is.

The whole problem of war would in truth be incredibly difficult of solution, were it not for one supreme fact, namely, that before a modern war breaks out the vast majority of all nations, all peoples – say, 99 per cent of them – fear and hate the very thought of it. When the psychologist first suggests to the airman that his quick terrors and trembling flesh are a result not so much of the gruelling experience he has come through as of some long-buried incident of childhood, the airman may be forgiven for feeling sceptical if not insulted. By evoking an unresolved ancestral memory, one man can lead ninety-nine against their normal desires upon what may prove the bloodiest courses. The long-buried, the unresolved thing may at any moment rise up and have us by the throat. To weaken its grip, to destroy its power, we have got to look at it, to know it for what exactly it is, to under-stand it. There is no other way of overcoming it.

So that if we thus regard tradition – and each country has its own tradition – in its worst aspect, upon its dark evil side, we are forced to conclude that the only way of getting rid of the evil is not by bombing it or running away from it, but by an analysis that leads to its clear understanding. Only through understanding do we achieve freedom.

Fortunately the study of tradition is not an unrelieved study of evil. On the contrary, it is largely a study of our highest good. Only inside his own tradition can a man realise his greatest potentiality; just as, quite literally, he can find words for his profoundest emotion only in his own native speech or language. This admits of no doubt, and literature, which is accepted as man's deepest expression of himself, is there to prove it.

Tradition would thus, on all counts, appear to be a very important thing indeed, for within it we realise our greatest potentialities for good and evil. Interfere with that tradition, try to supplant it by another tradition, and at once the creative potential is adversely affected. History shows that this admits of no exception.

Perhaps it is along some such line of thought that certain recent and somewhat sporadic movements in our own country may be finally under-stood. Let us see. I know, for example, that at the mere mention of such words as Scottish Renaissance or Scottish Nationalism there are at once aroused all sorts of mixed feelings, including wariness and much suspicion. I am not going to give myself away to the chance psycho-analyst. No fear. If he probes too far I am going to laugh and dodge. Yet in a calmer moment, if I have any intellectual curiosity left, I am bound to ask myself why these particular Scottish manifestations (or eruptions, or rashes, or as you will) should appear. They are symptoms – of what?

Let us try to examine them with the interested detachment of a psycho-analyst dealing with a case of shock. For the chances are that they do represent a state of illness, indeed almost precisely a state of shock inasmuch as the actuating irritant is buried so deep that it cannot be clearly discerned.

But first of all let us be sure that we have a fairly clear grasp of what we understand by tradition, or at least aspects of it upon which we can agree. What tradition means to each one of us in our blood is difficult to define. But how tradition has expressed itself outwardly we can at least see. And the two main ways of expression are through language and social institution. As the saying goes, we can tell a people by their literature and social institutions; for, given these, we know their tradition, the inmost feelings and impulses and aspirations by which they live and move and have their being. Now psychology has shown that you cannot supplant or destroy what is vital; you merely drive it into the dark deeps. This is the very important new knowledge that science has given us. A man can drive underground a vital experience of his past; a people can drive underground the vital part of their tradition; but the time comes when that which was driven under must come to the surface if life and health are to continue. A man can die. A people can die. But so long as a people, whose tradition has been driven underground, are not yet dead, they will in moments of crisis, of sickness, want to liberate their traditions so that they may have life abundantly again. And the two main symptoms of this condition will inevitably take the form of a desire for expression in language and in social institution, for a literary renaissance and a political nationalism. This does not merely apply to Scotland. It has applied to every country in Europe at one time or another.

Of course it may be unfortunate that all this should be the case, and some of us may find that the best way of getting over the trouble is by refusing to believe it. We proceed to have other ideas; in fact, we have other ideals. We fly off at a tangent with our ideals, those pale, abstracted, rootless, and therefore deadly things. There is a wise old Gaelic proverb which says: 'Whoever burns his bottom must himself sit on it.' But with our ideals we have persuaded ourselves that the basic fact, being politely unmentionable, need not be sat upon; or we can get an inferior people to sit upon it; or we can all stand; or, by much millennial aspiration, sprout wings and fly. Meantime, however, the poor fellow with the burn has to sit down. It's hard luck on him.

11

On Belief

I HAVE JUST BEEN READING a book called *I Believe*, containing 'the personal philosophies of twenty-three eminent men and women of our time'. As I turned
over the last few pages, where the work of some of these men and women is
advertised, I was struck by a success in sales which must surely throw a reflection on belief in general. Usually a remark about a best-seller is taken as refer-
ring to a novelist or one of his books. That need no longer be the case. Here are
books by so eminent a mathematician and social thinker as Bertrand Russell
running into their seventh, eight, and tenth impressions. H. J. Laski's *Grammar
of Politics* is in the seventh impression of its fourth edition. Lancelot Hogben's
Mathematics for the Millions is in its '150th thousand in English'. And so on. In
comparison with such figures, the works of many of our most eminent literary
men may be considered still-born. For example, of one of the contributors to
this volume, an editorial note says: 'E. M. Forster, since the death of D. H.
Lawrence, would probably by many critics be ranked as the foremost living
English novelist. He has attained his eminence by the production of few books
and these have generally reached only a small audience.' The truth would seem
to be that literature has gone out of fashion and popularisation of science and
political ideologies have taken its place.

It is with all the more interest, then, that we turn to the 'personal philosophies'
of these eminent men and women. And, looking for eminence, the eye inevitably
pauses first before that great name, Albert Einstein. 'The ideals,' says Einstein,

'which have always shone before me and filled me with the joy of living are goodness, beauty, and truth.'

And there, in words that have haunted the poet from the beginning of time, is summed up the path of what the others in varying ways – through religion to political materialism – strive to assert. That is what remains, after personal immortality is saluted or discredited, after God is seen to be a lingering tribal myth or the divine power that still animates the universe. It is in the light of that old conception of the meaning and worth of human life that totalitarian power, brutality, capitalism, cruelty, destitution, and, above all, war, are condemned. Here Professor J. B. S. Haldane says: 'My philosophy is the philosophy of Marx and Engels, of Lenin and Stalin.' He analyses the social condition of the world, goes through the Marxist creed, and optimistically hopes that we shall avoid the final disaster of Fascism on the one hand and a prolonged and bloody civil war, as in Russia, on the other, and, with the help of reason, carry the 'old culture into a new economic system'. To Bertrand Russell, 'Fascism and Communism, when analysed psychologically, are seen to be extraordinarily similar. They are both creeds by which ambitious politicians seek to concentrate in their own persons the power that has hitherto been divided between politicians and capitalists. Of course they have their differing ideologies. But an ideology is merely the politician's weapon; it is to him what the rifle is to the soldier.' For 'it is not by violence, cruelty and despotism that the happiness of mankind is secured'. And he brings history to witness.

So we have strophe and antistrophe, but always so that the profound human values, which it has been the business of literature to apprehend and vitalise in all lands, among all peoples, may come to flower in a stable society. Indeed, E. M. Forster, surrounded by 'militant creeds – in a world rent by racial and religious persecution – where ignorance rules, and science, who ought to have ruled, plays the subservient pimp' does not even believe in belief. 'I have, however, to live in an Age of Faith – the sort of thing I used to hear praised and recommended when I was a boy. It is damned unpleasant, really. It is bloody in every sense of the word. And I have to keep my end up in it. Where do I start?' He starts with personal relationships, the only comparatively solid thing left, and they require 'tolerance, good temper and sympathy'. 'Personal relations are despised to-day. They are regarded as bourgeois luxuries, as products of a time of fair weather which has now passed, and we are urged to get rid of them, and to dedicate ourselves to some movement or cause instead. I hate the idea of dying for a cause, and if I had to choose between betraying my country and betraying my friend, I hope I should have the guts to betray my country.'

But every essay has its moment of personal revelation. W. H. Auden, the young poet, starts the alphabetic series. He lists himself as a schoolmaster, and his paragraphs, tidily numbered and subdivided, set forth his beliefs on matters economic, educational, legislative, individual and social. It is a fair summary of what many believe to-day. We seem to have been reading it these last few years in some form or other almost everywhere. But of it all the opening sentence is what may remain in the mind; 'Goodness is easier to recognise than to define; only the greatest novelists can portray good people.'

And if we next take the word truth, there is nothing in this volume that touches the issue so closely as the article by Sir Arthur Keith, world famous for his researches in the antiquity of man, beginning: 'Deep in my heart I find a strange reluctance to set down here my innermost beliefs concerning God, man, and the universe.' These innermost beliefs are in themselves not unusual because they spring from scientific convictions and are held by perhaps the majority of scientists, but what is unusual is his sensitive concern for their expression where they might give offence or cause pain in the world of personal relationships. 'Allowances are made for me. The vicar of the parish, a man of my own age, is my nearest neighbour. We are on good terms – Church and chapel decorate our village. Life to be enjoyed has to be decorated. Bare subsistence is not enough.' He would be distressed were he to return a thousand years hence to find churches and churchmen swept from the face of Kent. 'This attitude of mine toward the church and to all forms of religion is a bone of contention between me and many of my fellow rationalists of England. Many of them are militant. "Is it not the duty of everyone," they demand, "to fight for the truth and to destroy error – in season and out of season?" On such occasions I am pacifist. I hold that truth has to make its way in its own right without browbeating. A forced truth, like a forced peace, has no enduring value.'

Tolerance, good temper, sympathy. Perhaps their clearest expression may be found in the contribution by the Chinese writer, Lin Yutang. 'A thing may be so logical you are convinced it must be wrong – The more complacent, self-satisfied and foolishly logical systems, like Hegel's philosophy of history and Calvin's doctrine of total depravity, arouse in me only a smile. On a still lower level, the political ideologies, like Fascism and Communism as they are usually represented to-day, seem to be but caricatures of thought – both are products of Western intellectualism and show to me a curious lack of self-restraint.' He quotes Confucius: 'There is no one who does not eat and drink, but few there are who really know flavour.' And Mencius: 'He who attends to his greater self becomes a great man, and he who attends to his smaller self becomes a small man.' In the chiefs of 'some of the Fascist nations' he sees 'images of beasts filled with greed and cunning and egotism.' Yet he refuses to admit that in the most warlike nations 'more than 1 per cent of the people, down in their hearts, welcome another war.' – an assertion that is worth pondering, and one which I, from experience, believe. When we all tend towards despair or cynicism, that conviction about the 1 per cent – surely within near reach of certainty – provides a solid anchor-hold for optimism. 'Science is but a sense of curiosity about life, religion is a sense of reverence for life, literature is a sense of wonder at life, art is a taste for life, while philosophy is an attitude towards life – '.

How assertive, almost shrill, sounds H. G. Wells against that background! Here we are at system-building and world-building again. But I have never been able to follow Mr. Wells into his higher social-speculative regions. Most of us must seem to him like bees who refuse to run our hive with the efficiency of real bees, though he demonstrates, complete with flower-seed packets, the only way to do it (even if his demonstrations change with the years). Jettisonning the immortal soul of the individual, he, however, believes in 'the immortal soul of the race'. 'Naturally my ideas of politics is an open conspiracy to hurry these tiresome, wasteful, evil things – nationality and war – out of existence.' He does not define the evil that resides in nationality. Is it implied that nationality is the sole cause of war? But later on he says: 'All war is not nationalist.' In fact in another moment he finds the war danger arising from 'a great release of human energy and a rapid dissolution of social classes, through the ever-increasing efficiency of economic organisation and the utilisation of mechanical power'. The terrific internal war in Russia was not nationalist, and if wholesome progressive countries like Norway and Denmark and Holland had had their wish they would have had less than nothing to do with this war. 'This world and its future is not for feeble folk any more than it is for selfish folk. It is not for the multitude but for the best,' says Mr. Wells. Who, among the present belligerents, proclaim themselves to be the best, the chosen people, fighting for the immortal soul of the race? I can feel this vague emotion of uplift toward finer things, but I still have to start from the actual ground under my feet. My nationality, as my particular background and heredity, is still very real to me. Just as its music – say, Gaelic music – is real to me. If someone said to me that Gaelic music, in its particularism, should be abolished as an evil in favour of some still-to-be-developed synthetic-symphonic form, I should simply feel bogged. To cut what is known and loved from under my feet and in the same breath to tell me to march is to require of a poor fellow, who knows himself as one of the multitude, an excessive nimbleness. If I had to choose between betraying my friend and betraying the immortal soul of the race, it would not require a great drain upon guts for me to plump for my friend. In short, I feel that Mr. Wells is playing a high earnest game with his head, and loves moving the pieces about on the board. But somehow I don't find a deep spiritual concern for these pieces, not a great deal of that 'elemental sense of piety or reverence for life', in Lin Yutang's phrase.

However, let us leave all strident crying about ideologies and systems, and, for refreshment, consider an altogether new kind of thought about this warring world. For Jules Romains there is always 'some aspect of the mind for reality to uncover, some aspect it has not discerned before, or which it has sized up badly. On the other hand, reality itself is changing more or less quickly. When the mind therefore is impeded by a system or a credo, it is really reduced to losing contact with reality'. And then: 'I believe that experience always has the last word – I shall never admit that reason should refuse to consider a fact of experience merely because it is improbable and contrary to the postulates of science to date. All the worse for science to date. Taking into account the new fact, it must simply begin anew its exposition of the nature of things. For example: perhaps some day two or three experiments only, but conducted under absolutely rigorous critical control, will demonstrate that certain persons in a particular psychic state are able to foresee and describe a future event in a way that excludes all possibility of explanation through coincidence, logical foresight, the realisation of some unconscious desire, or suggestion. When this happens, I hold that human reason will have to discard very nearly all its current ideas about time, space, causality, the determinism or indeterminism of phenomena, human free will, the nature of the soul and the cosmos. This would be the greatest revolution conceivable.'

In the Highlands we have long been used to this notion, as exemplified in second sight. In the Highlands, too, there has remained over from an old culture much of that elemental sense of piety or reverence for life. The spirit still has an instinctive urge to dodge restrictive mechanisms. It might even be an interesting and revealing exercise to attempt a psychological analysis of the peculiar native reaction to unemployment insurance stamps!

For it would seem clear that a system or ideology of the highest intention may in practice result in the most barbarous cruelty; that knowledge, as knowledge, obtained from a host of best-selling books on science and politics, may lead to an increasingly destructive materialism; unless, behind system and book, there is a concern for the living spirit of man, for those qualities that shone before Einstein and which it has always been literature's dedicated task to keep vivid and alive.

12

On Looking at Things

To keep the mind focused on danger or fear does not always help it when the critical moment arrives. There is much hysterical folly written these days around the word 'escape' or 'escapism'. Indeed there are persons who think it wrong to live outside a vague welter of sensational fear, as if to do so were in some way a betrayal.

We all in a certain measure understand this mood. But it can become a tyranny and a weakening. If a man is mud-stained, he does not take a mud-bath. When his eyes are tired he shuts them. We forever need contrast if we are to be strengthened or refreshed. A man who, in a flash of vision, sees the beauty in his aeroplane, will pilot her all the better for that instant of detachment. We are strong because of our resources gathered in moments other than the moment of conflict. And like the petrol tank our resources need constant refuelling.

All of which may seem like an apology for introducing so inconsequential a subject as the art of looking at a thing, the more so as I have no particular proficiency in the art myself. But at least I have got to that stage where I recognise it is an art, that is, something which has to be learned. Even with the artist, it is not enough for him to have an aptitude for seeing directly and vividly: the eye has to be trained for years, indeed all through his life, and its powers of exquisite observation seem inexhaustible. It is the same, of course, with the ear of the musician. Indeed those of us who are not musicians but merely like music know how long it can take for the ear to get even a moderate understanding of the musical import of a master.

But our concern here is neither with artist nor musician, but with the act, which is within everyman's compass, of looking consciously at a thing instead of glancing at it half-consciously. This may seem a very simple act, but as it requires a direct effort of the will, it can prove tedious. For at the back of it is the thought: why bother? Where's the point if one is not a professional artist? Besides, there are so many things to look at, most of them seen over and over again and therefore commonplace. In short, why cumber the already harassed mind with futile detail about the shape of a tree or the colour of a primrose or the flight of a blackbird? The whole affair is so trumpery that it is irritating, like the chatter of gossipy women when they meet or of sparrows. Besides, there is a lot of make-believe about it all, and in its high falutin form not a little of that artistic *blah* which seems pretty anaemic to a man who has a spot of real work to do.

This reaction of the busy man is understandable but quite wrong. Why? Because he is deliberately throwing away something which costs him nothing. By simply not training his eye to look at a thing, he is denying himself a whole realm of amusement and delight. For it is never a question here of educating the mind or improving the morals or becoming a better citizen or anything 'good' like that: it is purely an affair of pleasure, like the pleasure one gets from sound drink in contradistinction to bad drink *when one knows the difference*.

Of course, in a matter like drink, a man will pretend he knows the difference, simply because he would be ashamed to deny the quality of his palate and the immediate pleasure that comes from its use. Here he apprehends the point immediately and will stick, say, to his own brand of Scotch with conviction. I have seen a man do this who yet had no real knowledge of whisky from its various single malts to its innumerable blends. But I have heard another man question the barman in such fashion that I immediately recognised the trained palate. The first could be cheated by any wily barman, but not the second.

When it comes to wine, a man must, of course, be able to show discrimination almost as a matter of form; be able to use simple terms like full-bodied, thin, smooth, dry, with some conviction. I can remember a time when I modestly believed I could do some distinguishing in the matter of claret – until I was referred to a gentleman who, blindfold, could tell vintage and year.

In this matter of palate, then, we see the point of educating the sense of taste. We admit the extra and higher pleasures achieved by the connoisseur in drink, and we generally think of him as a man of taste and refinement. And very properly, because he would be the last to abuse the instrument of his pleasure. Restraint and judgement are inherent in its exercise. He is not going to kill the palate that presents him with his golden moments. He has grown wise.

But claret and whisky – especially whisky in these sad days – present one great difficulty in this matter of educating a sense, and that is their cost in cash. For most of us, it is insuperable. There is one sense, however – and probably the greatest of the five – whose exercise costs nothing, infringes no trade-union rules, is shared equally by capitalist and communist, animal, bird, and reptile. It is the one with which we are concerned.

Is there some special way, then, of looking at a thing?

A year or so ago I happened to be with a distinguished Scottish artist in a wooded burn in the wilds beneath Ben Nevis. It was a hot day and the chequer of shadows on the cool rock beneath the trees beside the clear running stream was very pleasant. The green leaves dimmed the light and gave a richness to the ferns. The water was crystal clear and in the course of ages had hollowed great basins out of the living rock into which it now swirled in clearly defined eddies of sheer surprise and of mathematical beauty. The greeny-blue rock had been worn to a remarkable smoothness and seemed to communicate its colouring to the water in the basins, so that they set a smile hovering over the thought of antique baths and woodland nymphs. Let us say that it was one of those places to which anyone might give a second glance.

I remarked that often a scene would come vividly back into my mind to which I was conscious of having given no particular attention at the moment of seeing it and that it might not be necessary consciously to impress a scene on the mind. But the artist said that I was quite wrong and that it was necessary to impress a scene on the mind if one desired really to possess it permanently. He instanced the scene we were looking at. 'You have not only to see it now in all its features, but you have deliberately to look at it in your mind tomorrow to make sure that it is still there, and again the day after.' Not until you had gone through this process could you be said to possess the scene in the sense that you possess a deposit in a bank.

He was, of course,. quite right, as anyone may find by making the experiment. And it does not require a great deal of effort to make the experiment once. But it requires effort. We have to use our eyes.

Well, supposing this is done, what then? In what consists the pleasure of having the scene firmly implanted in the mind? The answer to this is very difficult, because the nature of delight is insusceptible of precise definition. To a man who had never tasted a strawberry, we should find it difficult to communicate the flavour of the berry. Many of us may have experienced the boredom of being led round his vegetable garden by an enthusiastic amateur cultivator. But perhaps a time came when with a house of our own we were compelled to do something about growing vegetables for a home-made salad. The ground is laboriously dug, the straight rows made, the seeds covered in – and from that final moment our attitude to vegetable growing is completely changed. We soon begin a daily visit to see if the seeds are coming through. Any indications of cat-scrapes or sparrow-baths arouse strong indignation, accompanied not infrequently by murderous intentions. And at last – lo! the delicate green shoots appear. If a poet said that this was a miracle, the gardener would be justly incensed at so impersonal an assertion. It is a miracle certainly, but one for which the gardener feels more than a little responsible.

So now with this scene that one has deliberately made a personal possession. But as a scene in the mind is much more intangible than a solid lettuce in the garden, one must expect similar differentiation in the nature of the pleasure. And so it is. But the pleasure is there, in however slight a degree – to begin with.

Assuming, for example, one is a clerk in a city (to take a simple case). A day comes inevitably when one is bored. The same eternal round of desks and ledgers, of making entries, of totting up figures. Life is drab and dry as dust. There is no help now – except from one's own mind. But from this mind one can take out a pleasant cool scene of ferns and greeny-blue rock-basins where nymphs bathe. One glances up and out through the window at the sky. And if one cannot see the sky because of a nearby canyon wall, there is at least light on the wall, the sun's light – even though the sun itself be hidden. Does that help at all? Probably not, for it rouses only a deeper dissatisfaction with the office boredom. So delectable appears the remembered scene that its coolness and atmosphere of freedom do little more than irritate now.

Practising scales is not a happy business, and often enough one could smash the violin. But a time comes when the fingers fall correctly without effort, and the melody emerges.

As the eye becomes expert at looking at a thing, the laboriousness in registering the effect almost entirely disappears. In the hour of boredom, not one but a multitude of scenes are available for inspection. Though actually the affair is much more subtle than one of number. In our present world, a man with a large bank balance can (or could) walk along the street feeling fairly secure. He does not have to think of its extent; it is enough that it is there.

Now bank balances are perishable, like lettuces. Indeed one may look forward to growing a new lettuce but not always a new bank balance. The scenes, however, that are stored away in the mind are imperishable. You don't require to take them out and count them, unless you happen to feel in the mood for so specific and pleasant an exercise, because they have become part of you.

That seems a simple statement but in reality it is rather a tremendous one. The most notable thing about a man who makes a 300 break at billiards is the consummate ease with which he does it. The balls run to his bidding with a smooth obedience as if they were enchanted. So with the scenes, with the multitudinous forms and colours and substances of the world around, once they have really become part of the mind, of one's personality.

The mind now can, almost in any situation, achieve a certain detachment. It has fallen into the habit of seeing things with clear eyes. So out of his learning and habit of thought does the true scholar achieve detachment. With this detachment comes a singular feeling of confidence, of pleasure, and, too, of perpetual wonder. With this as a background, one can face up to the desperations of the world with some measure of steadiness and assurance, and perhaps with that quiet solitary sense of humour that is primordial and good.

13

On Magic

THE TROUBLE ABOUT MAGIC, AS about all old customs and superstitions, is our difficulty in appreciating the emotions of those who came under its influence. Where sympathy is lacking, understanding is not only incomplete but is also inclined to be critically destructive and even contemptuous. Many write of what they call the old superstitions as of a particularly horrible kind of ignorance from which an enlightened scientific age has mercifully freed us. There is, of course, some point and value in this attitude in so far as it is based on an innate desire, or instinct, for freedom. Where all is governed by necessity, absolute freedom must remain a notion or a myth; nevertheless, it is a notion whose fulfilment we grope after. And when stark logic, in front of what modern systems of thought call 'economic necessity', has to admit that absolute freedom is a myth, it tackles the conception of freedom itself from another angle, and considers that in the very act of recognising necessity we rise superior to it and so attain the only and the true freedom.

This is very nice, but not, for some mysterious reason, completely satisfying. For it is remarkable how the least prejudiced among us will often, in the face of clear logic, maintain an attitude of doubt. This new (and also very old) conception of freedom, arising out of the dialectical process, appears to have in it a certain casuistry, a certain hankering after a notion which yet, by definition, it expels. And this notion is, without doubt, the old magical content in our apprehension of that strange condition which man persists in calling freedom, *tout court.*

For the real trouble about logic is that it is inclined to repel or expel the purely emotional condition surrounding or interpenetrating that which it is about to examine. The logician is not concerned with the that we may have here; indeed, experience has told him to mistrust this feeling, as a contorting influence, at the outset.

Which is all very fine, and all very sound, when the business on hand is a scientific investigation of matter. The mathematician would certainly confuse the issue if he allowed any private feeling that one and one make three to interfere with his equations. In analysing the grey matter of the brain the physicist neither looks for nor expects to find our sense of beauty. The physicist and the chemist have a certain clear function to perform and they perform it with remarkable skill; but it is directed towards the physical side of our universe.

There remains the mental side, and here the scientific investigator works with materials and under conditions quite different from those of physicist and chemist. Here it is the feeling that is important, not the grey matter. In the act of drinking a glass of wine, we are content to be completely ignorant of its chemical composition – and no doubt some curious fellow has broken it up and analysed it. In fact, if such a curious fellow presented us with a glass of ruby liquid and said that it contained all the elements of a true port, what is the first thing we should do? We should, of course, sniff the wine, and if we found that the characteristic bouquet was lacking, we should shake our heads and decline the potion, saying: 'This may contain all the elements of a true port, but it is not port.'

So with any metaphysical concept or emotion: we may analyse them into what may be their factors, their elements, but if in so doing we lose their characteristic bouquet – the intangible something, the state of mind, out of which they were precipitated in the first instance – then we remain dissatisfied. It may be true that as creatures living in conditions of 'economic necessity' we cannot attain a state of individual freedom. It may be true that therefore the only proper concept of freedom is that which in the very act of recognising necessity becomes as it were freed from it (much as we become freed from the fear of lightning once we have understood its nature and set up a lightning conductor). It may be true, but we do not quite believe it, because it does not altogether tally with our feelings, because at times we have feelings of pure freedom and at other times feelings of pure necessity. We must eat: that is necessary. But we are not always eating.

Very well, says the economic determinist; let us so arrange our affairs that we have to devote the minimum of time to economic necessity and the maximum amount of time to what you call freedom; let us introduce a new social order with these aims in view.

What could be more desirable? But – the poor irrational fellow, cluttered about with his feelings, cocks an eye at the economic determinist. Can he trust him and his new social order? What about the fellows who are setting up new social orders all over Europe, with much shouting about freedom and the common good? They don't seem to him to be good enough. But if we could get right at the back of his mind, I fancy what we should find there is a suspicion that in any of the new orders he would feel trapped, that he would lose this curious, imponderable thing which he calls personal freedom, and which lies beyond reason, in the region of the irrational attitude, the magical thrill.

This may be extremely crass of him and superstitious. But he doesn't care about that. However difficult his 'economic necessity' at the moment, at least he feels that he has not got his head in a poke. His head is free – and that's something. The rest of the body will struggle out somehow.

Moreover, in the course of his varied history he has had a considerable experience of fellows with systems. In the simplicity of his heart he is enjoying, let us say, his reactions to Nature. Nature contains many remarkable and mysterious things and manifestations, and in his reactions to them he has had curiosity and wonder, fears and thrills. Along comes the witch-doctor who, for reasons best known to himself – and not unconnected with human power, gathers all the elements and reactions into a system of worship, and slowly turns the primordially hopeful and good into the fearful and bad, and, by propitiatory need, into at last the dark and bloody deed. The magical relation of man to his background, the white magic that is still the essence of art or lyric in its purest form, suffers a land change into dark superstition, into black magic.

All of which is not something that merely happened long ago. It is happening now, in one form or another, everywhere, from power politics to sex. The black magic of sex is perversion.

Turning up the pages of *Carmina Gadelica* to check a reference, I found myself some half-hour later lost in the account of what used to happen out in Uist on the eve of St Michael. It is a truly remarkable account of a festival by the common folk, given a whole meaning and cohesion by what we would call superstition. The very air seems full of magic. And the whole is steeped in a profound happiness and goodness. It is proper that every husbandman in the townsland should give, on the day of St Michael's Feast, a peck of meal, a quarter of struan, a quarter of lamb, a quarter of cheese, and a platter of butter to the poor and forlorn …' They ride in procession round the graves of their fathers and then hasten to the sports field. The riders in the horse races are without bonnets and shoes, in shirts and shorts. 'Occasionally girls compete with one another and sometimes with men.' On St Michael's night a great ball is held in every townland. Gifts are exchanged between young men and women. Song and dance, mirth and merriment 'are continued all night, many curious scenes being enacted, and many curious dances being performed, some of them in character'. Altogether there is a suggestion of eager life, a wonder upon things, a freshness in the eye, a vivid delight.

The leaves turn over, and my eye falls upon what happened to a famous violin player in the island of Eigg. 'He was known for his old-style airs, which died with him. A preacher denounced him, saying: "Thou art down there behind the door, thou miserable man with the grey hair, playing thine old fiddle with the cold hand without, and the devil's fire within." His family pressed the man to burn his fiddle and never to play again. … The voice of the old man faltered and the tear fell. He was never again seen to smile.' Presumably he thus attained freedom from his violin playing by recognising necessity under Divine Law.

So man naturally has grown a trifle wary about any denouncing of his superstitions. It so often happens to him, that what he takes delight in seems to be wrong, that he is beginning to doubt all witch-doctors, all leaders, and not a little even the conception of progress itself. For it is the fashion of the modern conception to be logical and scientific, while it is from the illogical, the irrational, that most of his fun and frolic, not to mention the profounder movements in his spirit, would seem to arise. The sea is a great mass of water of known composition from which he can get fish and in which he can drown. But in his sailing boat on a summer morning, the sea is much more to him than that. So with the wind; with trees, and mountains, and the shapes of valleys. In certain moments their contemplation moves him to extreme delight, even at times to something approaching ecstasy, so that, not caring a rap for witch-doctor and system, he will shout and dance and bubble with merriment.

Science may take from him the god of the sea, of the tree, of the mountain (though precious little, he realises at the height of his irrational moment, science knows about any sort of god, least of all the imagined one!), but when science tries to take away, or analyse away, the magical thrill, then let science either attend to its own proper business or go to the devil. And as for the witch-doctor, keep an ever more wary eye upon him. We don't hanker after any brand new system. All that most of us want is that those disabling factors (such as poverty and slums) which stand between us and our delight may be increasingly removed. We will take a long chance on 'progress' or 'improvements', if we are able to live more vividly, to experience the magic thrill of living out of which, so long ago, the one undying conception of freedom was born. In the most perfectly regulated hive, where economic necessity is the supreme law, the working bee has become a neuter.

14

On Destruction

WHEN I WAS A BOY we played Redskins. We were fierce and cunning warriors, and though we 'chose sides' and proceeded to consult together on major strategy, the subsequent action over wooded terrain was a highly individualist affair. We made our own laws covering the general conduct of operations and defining, in particular, when a man must account himself dead or captured. As, at a critical moment, we were all umpires, there was occasionally some difficulty in this matter of definition, and a dead man, feeling himself deeply injured, might be inclined to assert himself in a lively manner. The really important thing, however, was the achievement, by conjoint exercise of woodland craft and swift boldness, of a deed of derring-do. Our textbooks clearly exemplified the true nature of derring-do. They were often, perhaps, a little out of date, as we could never be certain of the financial resources to cover the cost of a regular 'order'. But the principles that guided both the moral conduct and the general prowess, against desperate odds, of the great hero, Buffalo Bill, never varied. When our parents referred to them as 'that trash' and refused them house-room, we accepted their ignorance and their ruling with the proper stoicism and turned a drystone dike or a byre-loft into 'a secret cache'. A bout of reading generated an idea and led to action. A book like *Tom Brown's School Days* would have bored us very much. But then we gravely suspected all books, perhaps not without reason, for we carried a few of them to school.

Something of this flashed back into my mind as the boy handed me a pistol the other evening. He had disposed two opposing armies of lead soldiers on the floor. One was guarding a fort which he had cleverly constructed out of empty cigarette boxes, and the other was deployed to capture the fort. I had to shoot his soldiers in the fort and he had to destroy my attacking troops. Shot about; and he politely handed me 'the first go'.

The deadly massacre proceeded ruthlessly, and when one side had been defeated to the last man, the troops were deployed again and a fresh battle started.

The excitement of the continuous action was heightened by graphic accounts of a recent film wherein, it appears, the Foreign Legion is exhibited in an engagement whose realism leaves nothing to fancy. The sounds of the rifle shots, and the different ways in which a man clutches at himself, reels and falls dead, were reproduced for my benefit with striking verisimilitude.

Naturally our conversation grew eager, but when I questioned a certain small military detail, he disposed of me at once, and that even without taking the poker or other convenient implement to represent a rifle. He performed his soldier's drill with an invisible rifle, and so precise were his arm movements that it required no effort of the imagination to see the rifle and hear the hand slap. Such perfection could have been achieved only after long concentration and effort, voluntarily undertaken. I am quite sure that when he is unable to perform this flawless drill in his dreams, he has nightmares.

And then I got a slight shock. I asked him, in the usual grown-up manner, what he would like to be, expecting to receive a picture of an officer leading his men against desperate odds, for he is a boy of courage and considerable resource. At football, I understand, he barges into a dangerous melee with complete enthusiasm. His physical courage and aptitude for swift decision make him a natural leader. But he replied to my question by saying that he would like to be a private soldier.

'No,' he answered a further question, 'I would not care to be an officer. An officer has great responsibilities, but a private – a private is free.'

Now I am quite sure that he did not acquire this point of view from anyone. It worked itself out purely in his boyish mind. It was a philosophic assessment of a situation known to many soldiers from experience.

To go into the point further would be to raise too many issues of deep psychological import. I would merely suggest that this apparent fear of responsibility implies neither weakness of character nor an absence of the natural ambition to excel. I found, for example, that this boy did fear 'a wrong order that would endanger the lives of others'. By 'others' he meant, of course, his 'comrades'. Already his social sense mistrusts a self-seeking destructive egotism.

But the point that first jumped to my mind was a very simple and practical one. I saw in a moment how little boys, excellent lads, shaping well for fine citizenship, could be used by a tyrant for purposes of mass destruction. Let the tyrant be represented as the Absolute One (the Father, according to Freud) and let 'the order' issuing from his responsibility be infallibly 'right', then the fight is on to the death, and all the more so should it have the 'glory' of being against 'desperate odds'. But how can the tyrant be made the Absolute One, and his orders right? The answer is: by propaganda working inclusively and subtly on the known elements of the child mind. The normal, healthy, balanced child already knows that an order of his own may be fallible, with disastrous results. He lives in a world where life and death orders are given. He therefore desires the infallible order. That alone will 'free' him from personal and social disaster.

Now add to that the fact that one of the strong elements in the child mind is an urge to destroy, an irresponsible urge, and a warlike situation becomes truly menacing. One begins to perceive that talk of wiping out a given civilisation need not be rhetorical.

This urge towards destruction that inhabits us comes out in many curious ways. I have a letter from a friend whose town has been recently fiercely bombed. He expected to be scared stiff, but actually found himself moved by 'a hellish curiosity'. One is prepared to take considerable risk to satisfy this curiosity.

When the mind wanders away by itself after such a piece of news, say, as the sinking of the *Hood*, does one come upon it indulging in an orgy of cunning counter-destruction? These phantasies of destruction, how common they must have become to us all! Phantasies of annihilating destruction! In the child mind, their proportions must occasionally be colossal.

And not only in the child mind. I have just read a novel by a distinguished writer which is devoted entirely to a period of strife – or revolution – in a remote country. The piling up of horror is so continuous that finally one is hardly moved, presumably because one is glutted. In the attitude of the writer himself, I fancy I detect a detachment that though continuously observant and curious, is spiritually weary and tainted by sadism. But I may be wrong.

Freud deals with what he supposes to be two opposite tendencies in man: the will to create and the will to destroy. The destructive instinct he finds in every living being and its object is apparently to overcome the living element and reduce it to inert matter. When this instinct cannot find satisfaction outwardly, it may turn inward, and after doing its best or worst with phantasies may set up a morbid or pathological condition. The only sure way of avoiding this morbid condition is by giving free play to the destructive impulse – or 'death instinct' as it has been called – in the outside world.

So the whole situation regarding the shooting of lead soldiers becomes extremely and ominously complicated.

But do not let us wander too readily into the realm of theory. We know what theory can do in the hands of a tyrant. We even know how man can be cursed and destroyed in the name of an ideal. When D. H. Lawrence mistrusts all idealisations, he may be sound. What is certain is that the practical application of an ideal to human affairs has often resulted in bloody tyranny. History records the fact. Let us hang on, quite simply, to facts and effects. In the name of communal brotherhood, it may be argued, brothers have to be slain. Argue away, but note very carefully the fact of the slaying. There is a destructive impulse somewhere in us and a creative impulse, but Freud's analysis is only an hypothesis.

Whatever the nature of, or reason for, the destructive impulse, we are quite sure that we don't want to be turned into inert matter. That is fact number one. The tyrant recognises it and tells his men that they are 'fighting for their lives'. Not even a megalomaniac would get men to fight for death. It may start as a fight for a special kind of life, a new order of existence, or what not, but in the actual struggle itself the issue is simplified to life or death, and then one fights 'for dear life'.

What I suddenly saw very clearly while knocking over the lead soldiers which were under the command of my young opponent (for ideally in this game he himself was the Absolute One) was that by a combination of elements and circumstances, such as I have here hinted at, the destructive impulse can be elevated into a predominant principle of action. Its capacity for destroying human life and creative human institutions then becomes colossal. The morbid phantasy is projected into the external world and made factual.

I am not, of course, here trying to establish a theory which most of us have already accepted. What was made clear to me was the actual *process* whereby the destructive is made dominant and becomes active on a vast scale. Until we understand and see clearly the process itself, we will never understand how to set about organising and elevating the creative impulse, which is its opposite and which is stronger than it. (Were it not stronger, we should have disappeared off this earth long ago.)

Let me go back to my old Redskins. Actually our bouts of deathly tracking and hunting were sporadic and frequently had about them an air of play-acting, especially when accompanied by blood-curdling whoops. But all through our young lives there was contact with sea and land, with fish and fur and feather, sun and rain and mud and misery and happiness. Against that large and natural background of varied living and adventure in a considerable degree of freedom, the Redskins occupied a very minor part. They were something imported, and perhaps well designed to set off the superior cunning of the hunter, of primeval man out after food.

Anyway, I am quite certain that the boy whose thoughts are occupied by drill and lead soldiers, could have them diverted to other natural and boyish pursuits with equal intensity and far greater delight. For the delight in life has always been greater than the delight in death, and the creative impulse satisfies more finely the natural organism than does the destructive.

How to set about organising the creative impulse is another matter, and one that would require not only an understanding of the psychological elements involved but also of the economic and other institutions which man has produced. But such an understanding is also required by the tyrant who organises the destructive impulse, and we see him at work both on the child mind and the economic institution. His technique is worth the closest study, and evidence of his fell work is as near as the shadow that falls across lead soldiers and the head of a little boy in a remote and quiet living-room.

15

The New Community of Iona

A LOT OF CONTROVERSY HAS arisen around the effort by Dr George F MacLeod to establish on Iona a community of students of the Church of Scotland. The immediate hope,' he wrote in the Press in the spring of this year, 'is that some twenty students every year will, on completion of their course, and after licence, pledge themselves for two years to a community whose summer centre will be a log hut settlement within the Abbey grounds of Iona. They will study the peculiar modern task that faces us and the best approach to meet it; and half the day will be spent in manual labour. The very stones of the Abbey cry out to be rebuilded to form the permanent home of the new alignment. But each October the members will lay down pick and trowel and go off, two by two, to work in the housing schemes under the complete direction of their parish ministers. At the end of the two years' contact they will normally apply for a parish in the usual way.'

In short, the aim seemed to be a deliberate effort to revive in a small way the old Columban idea of fellowship, communal labour and ministry, together with a realisation of what we call 'modern conditions', and of the urgent need within the Church of Scotland itself for a revivifying impulse.

As a non-churchman, I offer my own opinions on this project with the utmost diffidence; yet as a Scotsman, aware in some measure of the influences and forces that made our country, I am perhaps entitled to offer some criticism of any attempt to interfere with historic evidence, even if such evidence be no more than a ruin, a tomb, a standing stone. The spiritual heritage of a people is the most real thing about them, and all the institutions they have formed have been instruments for its expression, in church or law or social custom. It is their tradition. It is that which distinguishes them from another people. Through it and it only can they express themselves to the full; can they draw from life its profoundest savour, its deepest meanings. To interfere with this heritage in a harmful or destructive way is to limit the full expression of each individual. Whereupon the whole people suffer, and that which they created of spiritual value tends to decay, and the common stock of humanity – its civilisation, its culture, call it what you will – is diminished at least to the degree in which the contribution of that people was unique. You have only to study the history of Scotland in the last century or two to appreciate in how precise a way this is true. The very fact that Dr MacLeod should find it necessary, in his special province of the Church, to attempt so seemingly romantic or extravagant a revival of fellowship and faith amidst his own brethren and amidst the Scottish people is surely in itself illuminating.

Accordingly, he was bound to meet both with opposition and with complete indifference. Indifference we may ignore here, for, by the very nature of the given circumstances, it is inevitable. Opposition tends to take three forms.

First of all, there are those who object to any interference with so important a ruin as the Abbey of Iona. They call it sacrilege and see in Dr MacLeod a man who wants publicity at any price. For, they argue, if this man desires an immortal name for himself let him go and organise his fellowship in the distressed areas of our land, let him gird up his loins and sally forth, through dangers and tribulations, as his inspired master, Columba, did fourteen hundred years ago. This battening on an established tradition of pilgrimage to the Holy Isle is too easy. And, further, it will destroy the inspirational force of these old stone ruins that time, under the hand of God, has weathered to a deeper, more universal purpose than they served even in their architectural prime. Twenty thousand pilgrims a year must deplore this attempt at sacrilege by an individual too obviously anxious to gain some personal notoriety.

I have here been trying to summarise some of the objections I have come upon in the Press. I do not know Dr MacLeod and can testify neither to a personal romanticism nor a desire for publicity. And I feel I can appreciate in some degree the spirit that informs this particular sort of criticism. For I know Iona well, have come under its spell of light and of history, and have the haunting feeling that I should like to go back to it at any time and find once again its incomparable peace and quiet.

Yet that feeling and those objections, I realise quite clearly, partake of the death instinct. We do not need to read Freud to understand this. Why, let us ask ourselves, has Scottish scholarship got such a deep antiquarian bias? Study its endless quarrels over historical minutiae. Whole societies can be roused to bitter personalities over whether it is proper or not to wear a certain sort of tie – or is it a waistcoat? – with a dress kilt. We are in love with our past because we are not conscious of a creative present. It is the death instinct at work in our heritage, calling defeatism by soft names, hanging on to some lovely thing – or thing our nostalgia has made lovely – to the point of rather seeing it perish than having it touched by any hand, least of all the creator's.

For consider how groundless these objections are even historically. Columba's settlement of wattle-and-daub huts and wooden church have completely disappeared. These ruined walls were the work of builders many centuries later. Their monastic function was not that conceived by Columba. The history of Saxon Margaret's influence in this island is worth investigating over against the organisation of that early Celtic Church. But however that may be, these ruins are not Columba's. They represent buildings used to carry on Columba's chief message. If Dr MacLeod thinks he can reconstruct them for the same purpose, he is at least fulfilling their traditional function.

Secondly, the notion of Columba as a missionary sallying forth into the unknown and settling by pure chance on a little island off our barbarian shores sounds very adventurous and heroic, but I doubt if that was the way it actually happened. In 1560 the Synod of Argyll destroyed 360 sculptured stones of Iona on the plea that they were 'monuments of idolatrie'. That Columba and his brethren of the wattle-and-daub huts, or their successors, erected these 'standing stones' is extremely unlikely. From some knowledge of early history or pre-history, we may confidently assume that they belonged to a vastly older age, Druidic and pre-Druidic. In a word, Iona was probably a religious centre of some importance at least a millennium before Columba landed on it. In view of the existence of Dalriada, he was bound to have known this and to have made use of it, with all the persuasive wisdom these early Christians showed towards the tolerant pagans they came amongst. If Dr MacLeod is trying to take advantage of a given religious atmosphere in Iona to assist his new missionary enterprise, he is merely following the general strategy of the far-seeing Columcille.

The second objection is concerned with what is deemed the artificiality and futility (not to mention heresy) of setting up a Christian brotherhood on Iona at this time of day, as if 'cowled monks chanting again in solitude; a community withdrawn from the snares of the world' were contemplated. But manifestly this is not what is contemplated. On the contrary, the scheme would appear to follow, in however small a way, the authentic Columban inspiration. Young men will meet here in brotherhood, will toil with their hands and have the communion of fellowship before setting out to bring what understanding and selfless devotion they may have learned to their brothers in the derelict areas of our civilisation. There is nothing unreal or heretical about this. Even in the matter of secular education the Danes have a parallel in their folk schools, where men and women of over eighteen meet and learn, and wash up their dishes and make their beds. It is the very ancient ideal of brotherhood and service, and the world would be none the worse of a lesson in its potency from whatever source, religious, educational, or political.

The third objection is raised by those who feel that as the religion of the churches is played out anyway, such an effort as Dr MacLeod's should merely be scorned. The 'progressive thinker' need have no fear of its 'reactionary tendencies'. It is the staging of a costume-piece and about as far removed from the realities of life as a millionaire is from the effects of the dole.

Now this objection is the only real one of the three, not in its direct criticism of the Church so much as in what is implied by its attitude. It is the attitude of those who feel they have not only something to say but something very positive to do. Dr MacLeod has referred to the 'lesser creeds' of Communism and Fascism. Let him consider for a moment what moves in the heart of the ardent young Communist or Socialist in our own country to-day. Never mind for the moment whether he is right or wrong; the important thing – as no churchman needs to be told – is what he believes. And his belief is the ancient one of brotherhood and justice between men. He sees that the ideal of brotherhood and justice has been betrayed. He can state the extent of the betrayal not merely in an impassioned logic but in a display of statistics where horror and degradation are worked out to an incontrovertible decimal point. And he accuses the Church of having allowed the betrayal to continue: nay, of having, by complacency, indirect action, and its own desire to retain power, assisted in the betrayal.

Those who accuse Dr MacLeod of envisaging something soft and easy when contrasted with the rigorous life of the Columban brotherhood can have hardly worked out the realities of the situation. It was probably softer and easier for the ancient missionary to preach amongst the groves of the pagan Picts than for his modern descendant to hope to move effectively amongst the slag heaps of our age. Assuming always, of course, that the modern is prepared to do it with the same zeal and self-denial and charity and faith.

Why should a non-churchman, like myself, be concerned about this one way or another? It is difficult to answer in a few words. But I think it might be said briefly that he is aware of an ever-decreasing amount of spirituality in the modern world. The increasing mechanisation of life, the loss of individual freedom under political tyrannies, the suppression of original thought and the manufacture by the Press of a public opinion – everywhere massed force, under a lust of power or a psychosis of fear, is robbing man of his dignity and life of its ecstasy, its profoundest delight. It is not inconceivable to forecast a rigid condition of affairs when little colonies of persons, secretly, will once more, in the old phrase, go out into the desert, to save man's spiritual life from extinction. And by spiritual life I mean the striving towards the achievement of harmony in the mind, that condition of synthesis, of fulfilment, which all the religious leaders and mystics and poets have striven for throughout the human history of our planet; which the scientist searches for in the constitution of matter; and which Columba knew so profoundly as a state of light.

Iona is the island of light.

From Iona this light, this vision without which the people perish, might in some measure be made manifest again. That Scotsmen should attempt the effort is logically sound, for they will start with a tradition and environment that is their heritage, physical and spiritual. But whether this particular new Iona Community will be able to rise above a narrow sectarianism, an effort to resuscitate their own particular church, with its conventional trappings and exclusiveness and conceptions of a jealous God, is another matter. Were it not for the existence of Iona itself, I should, perhaps, doubt it. But then strange miracles of light were wrought long ago on that small island in the Western Sea.

16
The Heron's Legs

SECOND SIGHT, MAGICAL CHARMS, INCANTATIONS, apparitions, other states of mind – the Highlands are as full of them as of scenery. Years ago or yesterday, a strange happening, an etched scene. What does all this odd traffic amount to? Whence – and whither? The same old questions, but with the old answers becoming less positive, the explanations less satisfying, even as the old scientist's final 'final indivisible particle of matter' becomes a spot of energy that jumps its location in an inexplicable way and leaves at least some scientists now talking of a substratum where the ultimate spot may be either material or mental, with emphasis possibly on the mental.

Superstition, I find myself involuntarily turning up the dictionary, not for a definition of the word, which I fancy I know, but for its root. And its root means to stand over or above. Which is exactly what happens at the moment of experiencing the odd happening or 'other' state of mind. One comes upon oneself standing there with a feeling of intense reality.

I am not concerned here with attempting 'final answers' to anything, for the excellent and even cheerful reason that I don't know them. And, anyway, unless the experiencing comes first, the knowing amounts to nothing. But there is this Highland background, so the Highland mind, being notoriously inquisitive, begins to wonder what happens beyond its own territory, within other countries, in this matter of unusual states of mind; and, to begin with, even in so elementary a thing as scenery.

A southern poet has said he could stand and stare. That's something. Vague a bit, but the stance is right. To ask what he is staring at might be like asking the point in a joke. Never mind. One asks. For here one must ask anything and everything with cheerful ruthlessness. Did the fellow see anything when he stared, inside him or outside, and if so what, more or less, was it? You don't destroy a wine by discussing its bouquet. So – was there anything beyond? After all, we know our way about this old territory. We are not going to be put off by the pretty-pretty or the vague that peters out. We know the English countryside. And so on – until Wordsworth suddenly says:

> I heard among the solitary hills
>
> Low breathings coming after me…

Now the Highlander is caught, and doesn't become more comfortable when Wordsworth takes his stance:

> …I would stand,
>
> Beneath some rock, listening to sounds that are
>
> The ghostly language of the ancient earth,
>
> Or make their dim abode in distant winds.

The Englishman even goes on to use the word 'audible':

> … in all things new
>
> I saw one life, and felt that it was joy.
>
> One song they sang, and it was audible …

But even when it comes down to specific bits of scenery, he is no less troubling. How often in the wilds of the Highlands I have filled a kettle from a burn and happening to look up and around, in that half-light which isolates, the grey light of magical suspension amid the fresh tingling earth scents … the remote cry of a hill bird … have seen the arch of the bridge at hand as a suddenly frozen frame for the picture. 'The lifeless arch of stones in air suspended', says Wordsworth. That glimpse of the lifeless, like the first glimpse of a 'frozen' hare.

So 'the sight' is not peculiar to the Highlands. Indeed if we went beyond Wordsworth to William Blake we would find it in full flow in the sense that human figures, invisible to others, would, as they passed by on the street, receive his salute. In fact, if I may trust my memory, he sometimes took them home to dinner and had long talks with them afterwards. And I suspect that their after-dinner speeches were not of the kind with which in the ordinary way we are familiar. But that is taking us too far ben in the Highland mental home. For the moment we are concerned only with bits of scenery, the elementary beginnings, the things we take so much for granted that we pass by without seeing them.

Let me try another country, and as Wordsworth has spoken of 'one life' that was 'joy' – an obvious unity for him, or even Unity in the full Eastern sense – let us go as far East as possible, to Japan.

As it happens, I have been in correspondence with Professor Nakamura, who deals with English in Tokyo University and is particularly interested in Scottish literature. But apart from such evidence of impeccable taste, what interested me was an early observation of his to the effect that life in the Highlands, as described in certain novels, reminded him of his own boyhood in Japan. This, I confess, astonished me, like the arch of the bridge. East is East, we had been told, and West is West, and never the twain shall meet. But here, bless us, was the bridge. Its arch was thrown over.

Not only that, for he next introduced what was an old Highland custom, one still observed on particular occasions. In brief, he assured me that in his land it was customary, on the occasion of a first special visit, to bring a gift. In due course it arrived, a recently published volume de luxe of early Japanese art.

Now I knew nothing about Japanese art, apart from those commercial prints of moons and cherry blossom, though even these had the kind of arrestment or suspension in mid air that had made me look at them more than once. But my extra difficulty with the large Japanese volume was, of course, that I could not read the letterpress, those ideograms, so fascinating to stare at. I often stared at them, noted their arrangement and order, and wondered what, in the realm of practical sense or information, they so mysteriously veiled. But then I could remember having done that with the lines that my remote ancestors had scrawled on stones. Once when I had stared at a bit of ogham script long enough I saw the primitive hand at work; and the primitive in action is a vividly potent force.

However, I had caught a glimpse, in the modern way, of what Eastern ideograms could represent, from a cosmopolitan like Ezra Pound, who had, among other things, done some translating. In particular, one Chinese poem comes to mind, and though, without the book, I could not reproduce a line of it, its impact is still fresh. Entitled 'The Exile's Letter', it evoked for me the Highland scene, with memories of two Highlanders, close friends, meeting at ceilidhs, having drinks, and parting. The texture, the feel, of the whole thing was somehow as familiar as the smell of peat smoke. In 'The Canadian Boatsong', evocative phrases like 'the lone shieling' or 'the misty island' gather potency because the rowers were exiles from their fathers' land. Uprooted. The far-wandering, the exile – half the history of any Highland clachan.

But to leave verse or words and come back to these Japanese paintings, for which I was given no words: or, even better, to real prints, not the commercial ones. Through the generosity, which is inexpressible, of my learned correspondent, I became the possessor of two coloured prints, one by Harunobu and the other by Hiroshige. In my ignorance, I wondered if these names might be mentioned in a recent issue of the Encyclopaedia Britannica, and on turning up the section dealing with Japanese painting I found not only the names but reproductions of their work. I was among the old masters of Japan. Here, anyhow, was something quite different from the Highland scene, so different that at first glance I found them attractive. Rather foreign of course, but quite attractive. Like that.

Then I began to look at Harunobu, from time to time. A pretty scene of two figures, plum blossom and a wooden fence. The figures have flowing draperies, and one is up on the fence cutting off a branch of blossom for the other. Lovers, presumably, though the ovals of their faces, with only a line or two to show they are faces, suggest neither sex nor emotion. It took me quite a time to notice the fence consciously, though actually it was more highly coloured than the rest, and when I did I began to wonder why its solid square posts, and the squares made by the two wooden horizontals, the whole running off the diagonal into the heart of the picture, did not disrupt it; for up above were flowing lines, blossom, and, containing them as it were, what looked like a meandering timeless river.

I can find no disruption. I think of an ancient monk doing an initial letter for the Book of Kells. At the odd moment when wireless reception is good in the Highlands, something from Mozart comes over clear. As a still rarer moment, I am visited by the exciting if not revolutionary notion that perfection may not be dull; even that it dwells beyond the exciting and revolutionary, like the plum blossom.

But that, again, is going beyond bits of scenery. So may I mention a third print in order to bring back the Highland scene, this time not with the troubling 'sight', but with the rarer serenity that, like the perfection of Harunobu's art, has delight at its core?

It is a picture of a heron, by Tanan (early sixteenth century). Now I have seen herons in many places of the Highlands, on pine trees or slowly, deliberately wading, but to come upon the bird in the evening, the solitary bird, almost to its knees in the water, still as a slender tree stump, fishing, its size magnified in the fading light, stops me in my stance, as if I had come upon more than the bird in that quiet place. This is the moment that is never forgotten.

Tanan has painted that bird, realistic to the fishing eye so sharply in its head. Yet when I look closely at the head the whole top half of it is one marvellous brush stroke. And the beak is another – a deadly spear. In the grey light, with a reed and a broken reed. Such economy of means, each stroke so inevitable, so final. A glance – and lonely Highland places do not have to be remembered in order to evoke the breath-taking wonder of having been there.

Can this wonder, and the serenity in which it lingers, be caught in words? Can it be set down, written, with the ultimate inspired simplicity, economy, of the single brush stroke? For me it was so caught when, unexpectedly as one comes upon the solitary heron, I came upon this poem out of the ideograms:

> With the evening breeze
>
> The water laps against
>
> The heron's legs.

17
The Flash

KEEP SILENT AND STILL AND watch what happens. This is a trick that has got to be learned, as the bird watcher knows when he hopes to record the new and surprising. Something of this I tried to indicate in my last article, when I came on the heron fishing a quiet stretch of a Highland river.

This experience was brought vividly back to mind, however, not by another such Highland experience on anyone's part, but by a Japanese painting of a heron. Here was something added to the 'new and surprising'. That a foreigner should see what I fancied I had seen and then fix it for good in a master's painting! In one sweep of his brush, what might be considered the local, the provincial, had vanished. It was certainly a silent comment on any small nation preoccupied with, say, its literature, to a degree that may occasionally be more than noisy, and certainly hopeless for bird watching.

But there was a shift here, a shift from the natural scene, the scene in nature, to the scene in the painting. The heron so to speak was beginning to occupy a scene behind my eyes. And in this mental scenery, as it opened out, I began to catch a glimpse of something more new and surprising than is normally observable in the realm of birds.

Now this something is very elusive, and as the rest of these articles are concerned with trying to get a glimpse of it from various angles, let me begin at the beginning with ordinary visual scenery. I had established a certain correspondence between the Highland way of looking at a heron and the Japanese way. Pictorially at least here was some accord. I had something to go on. But when I ventured into the realm of the Japanese mind, the scenery was so different from what I had been accustomed to that I found myself lost.

Normally at this point one gets back into the old familiar places as quickly as possible. But if the surprise, the shock, of finding oneself in such new and surprising scenery is great enough, there may be induced the involuntary reflection: That I should be here! I – here – amid the strange and bewildering! At such a moment, if the shock has really been astonishing enough, the 'I' has a new feel, a new taste. It is in a way as if one had never really met this 'I' before. It is suddenly isolated, new born – and the strange or bewildering element of the familiar in it makes its newness more felt. New born, or born again – as an apparition is born, magically. And coming upon an apparition is so rare an experience that it is unforgettable.

I am aware that this effort to be as precise as I know how may seem anything but, for in the ordinary way of living we imagine that 'I' is the one thing that is always with us, that we know it only too well, that we are forever being exhilarated by it, or betrayed, or bored to death.

As this is the kind of paradox I have been trying to resolve for a long time, and as I concern myself with its importance here, may I revert once more to the natural scene that included the heron, so that I may check what was written spontaneously about it. When I came upon the fishing heron I was stopped in my stance, I wrote, 'as if I had come upon more than the bird in that quiet place. This is the moment that is never forgotten'. I had been reluctant, I can now see, to say that the 'more' included, as its most surprising element, myself. And the reluctance sprang no doubt from sympathy or consideration for the reader, upon whom one can hardly unload a dubious or egoistical subjective experience. Let it be hinted at, and pass on. And don't now begin to go all self-conscious about it

All of which is beside the point, almost meaningless; even this use of the word 'self-conscious' is so ironically a misuse that one can do little but, as it is said, smile. For the real point of the experience is that one comes upon oneself, the 'I', as one may never have done before, almost as though it were outside oneself, in a detachment evoked by the strangeness of the scene and the moment. In this sense it is objective, not subjective. One apprehends one's presence there as one might the presence of a stranger. And the experience is incredibly refreshing, cool as birch-scented air, and full of wonder.

If I may appear to have over-elaborated all this it is in an effort to indicate the only kind of unusual instrument I had with which to tackle certain Eastern modes of thought or states of being. So now let me forget it, while I attempt to get a practical bearing on the Eastern modes and states which finally led me to what is called the Great Doctrine.

My first difficulty in this mental country was catching a glimpse of half a bearing before it disappeared. I soon realised that the logical process, as we know it, was of little use here, for it goes on from one thing to another, as cause to effect; it seems linear, one-dimensional, continues like a straight line, adding to itself until it is stopped by a QED, and so fulfils itself.

But nothing seemed to stop in this Eastern mode of thinking. It was never a case of a thing being either correct or incorrect; not even altogether of its being both at the same time, which could be absurd and therefore amusing. Far from having an absurd air, the Eastern performer was like one of those bland jugglers who keeps any number of things – balls, plates, clubs – whirling around him, flawlessly; as in the case of those more complicated atoms which our scientists sometimes condescend to set in toylike motion in order to help our understanding. But throw a QED spanner into the scientist's whirling toy and at that moment it would not fulfil itself, it would collapse.

To make things more difficult I had to think of the juggler as a living nucleus at the centre of his sphere of whirling electronic thoughts or apprehensions; as a living organism in action. And so I began to stumble towards the notion that this Eastern way of thinking was not linear, one dimensional, logical, but somehow three dimensional and organismal.

Now this was more than a trifle disturbing, because it interfered with security, with so to speak the welfare state of the mind. When our ideas are stopped being handed to us on a plate, where are we? When our Western ways of thinking, and all the psychological analyses of them on which we can lay hands, do not meet the Eastern occasion, what next? I confess my own instinctive reaction is at once to take cover behind the outworks that our science has made so marvellously available for sniping from. Let every idea or notion from an illogical or irrational outside be shot at, picked off, by a bullet from a rifle that works logically. It is bad enough when the physical welfare state is called in question, but the mental! So let me give our all-inclusive Science a capital initial, even at the risk of making it seem our god and scientific materialism our creed. One has got to have some sort of certainty in this warfare.

Yet at once, in this secure region, the word 'certainty' evokes by association that 'uncertainty principle' which has been troubling our physicists for some time. From certainty to uncertainty about the behaviour of specific things, actual things that can be manipulated, like the infinitesimals of matter, and manipulated so potently that any day now they may blow our whole secure world to smithereens.

I gathered that the words 'uncertainty principle' were like a gift to mentalists, mystics, and those who so think or think they fundamentally understand. Clearly one has got to be particularly careful here, because a vague state of mind about 'ultimates' can induce an emotional colouring or comforting that is wonderfully satisfying – as psychoanalysis has done its best to show. So let me hang on for a minute to what I conceive to be our logical approach to this uncertainty.

To quote scientists in the context where the uncertainty principle has its innings would not be difficult, for they have done their lucid best to make it intelligible to a groping layman like myself. Let that be taken for granted, while I go on to show the difficulty I experienced over what may seem a simple enough matter to many but which, from the logical viewpoint, rather stumped me. Difficulties over position and velocity of an electron, for example, I was pleased to leave to the scientist concerned with limitations to our possible knowledge, but the nature of the electron interested me because it seemed to involve an illogicality. Under one experimental set-up it was a particle; under another it was a wave. I could throw a pebble into a pond and set up waves on the pond. In this old pictorial way of under-standing, I perceived a difference between the pebble and the waves. Clearly the pictorial method in the new context was as out of date as the billiard balls or pebbles of the old mechanics. In short, I had to ask myself could one thing be two different things at the same time in this strange world of the infinitesimal electron. Then listening-in one night to a radio discussion among experts in different fields of knowledge, I was interested to hear the mathematical physicist explaining that though he appreciated the difficulty here in terms of the old classical logic, he found no difficulty in terms of mathematical logic which could produce an equation to cover or include such 'contrary' manifestations on the part of the electron. And the equation worked.

Now I seemed to find a distinction or difference between classical logic and mathematical logic, much as physicists to-day distinguish between classical mechanics and quantum mechanics. It is not a case of saying, if I dimly apprehend the matter, that the laws of classical mechanics are 'wrong' but of saying that they are not sufficiently inclusive of reality, as we now under-stand it, to cover whatever laws operate down among the infinitesimals of matter.

After such gropings, I decided that I could not reasonably apply my notion of western logic to Eastern ways of thought and confidently demolish such ways if they appeared to run counter to my logic. It was even more unsettling than that, for the more I pursued the matter the more I found that what were logical absolutes to me were no more than different aspects of reality to the Eastern psychologist, much as particles and waves were different aspects of an electron to our physicist. It was still more unsettling when I realised that what had long appeared to be absolutes to us were now, among the infinitesimals, not only 'aspects' but 'complementary'. It almost began to look as if our physicists, dealing with the ultimate reaches of matter, were beginning to set up some sort of comparison or analogy with the Eastern thinker dealing with the ultimate reaches of mind. And if I had a tremendous respect for our physicist, could I have less for the other who, after all, had been working in his realm for an extra millennium or two?

One further point here. Hunting for what ammunition I could find to deal with the East, I came across *Science and the Modern World,* by A. N. Whitehead. Here the distinguished mathematical logician, in searching for a new look at the ultimates of matter, decides on the evidence that the old doctrine of scientific materialism has to be abandoned in favour of 'an alternative philosophy of science in which organism takes the place of matter'. And if such a quotation may be unpardonably brief from so vast a range of thought, at least that word organism looked back at me from the page in *a way* that evoked my picture of the Eastern juggler.

But did all this elementary rooting among Western ways of thought help me any when at last I came in contact with the Great Doctrine? It did not. I simply got lost. Nor did it help when I discovered that any master of the Doctrine, Zen master, refused to talk about it on the basis that words were futile and misleading. Apparently it was no good asking how on earth one could understand without words, without reasoned expositions. To get knocked out in the ring is natural enough, but to get knocked out before one enters! So I cast around for anything that would provide some sort of insight and found a book called *The Zen Doctrine of No-Mind*, by D. T. Suzuki.

First, no words; next, no-mind. I began to feel like the old Highland reiver who decided he might as well be hanged for a sheep as a lamb. I even suspected that no-mind had some sort of specific, even technical meaning, denoting the state of mind that results when there is no mind in it. Which sounded Highland enough. And as for our modern semantics, didn't Confucius remark, some 600BC, 'If language is not correct, then what is said is not what is meant'?

So where was I? And where were my tentative pokings into the nature of logic when Dr Suzuki observed, 'All we can state about Zen is that its uniqueness lies in its irrationality or its passing beyond our logical comprehension'? Soon I was prepared to admit this fully. So perhaps I was not completely lost because I knew I was lost. Was this a conceivable angle of approach? And Zen itself? 'There is a school of Buddhism known as Zen. It claims to transmit the quintessence of Buddhist teaching ...' I had once tried to understand the ordinary teaching and given up. So everything was shaping well. I should soon be in the delicious middle of pure incoherency. And I was, for I got finally sunk in that ultimate experience of Zen called *satori*. Here is one of Dr Suzuki's simpler attempts to make this remarkable mental state clear to our Western minds: 'Satori makes the Unconscious articulate. And the articulated Unconscious expresses itself in terms of logic incoherently but most eloquently from the Zen point of view. This "incoherency" is Zen.' And this Unconscious, let it be plain, was far from being Freud's.

Why this began to affect me with delight I hardly knew, though I knew, too, that it was not altogether because of its 'incoherency', or, as we might say, absurdity. Nor was the delight lessened when a Zen master's aphorism reached my mental condition: 'In walking, just walk. In sitting, just sit. Above all, don't wobble.' I fancied I saw his eyes, and suddenly remembered Yeats and his lines on three Chinamen as they stare down, from the hillside they are climbing, upon 'all the tragic scene', with one asking 'for mournful melodies'. As the accomplished fingers begin to play.

Their eyes mid many wrinkles, their eyes,

Their ancient, glittering eyes, are gay.

And I knew that among all the poets of our modern age Yeats alone could have achieved that final 'gay'.

However, it is far from my intention or ability even to suggest the scope of Zen or what living by Zen means, with its difficult conceptions of morality, immortality, eternity. As for our unending torrents of words, our philosophical systems, our gargantuan Joycean outpourings, I caught a glimpse of a Zen master being affected by them as by a verbal diarrhoea that only silence could effectively medicate.

But perhaps I have suggested enough to indicate how one Highlander got lost in a new way of thinking that concerned the essence of being alive. Yet that may be a trifle misleading, because I fancied I followed Dr Suzuki through some of his books with reasonable intelligence, as indeed one should for he uses our Western philosophical modes of communication with a skill and an analytical subtlety that are fascinating. But though I knew in this fashion I also knew that I did not understand. At once the difference between knowing and understanding assumed crucial importance. Digging into past experiences for possible enlightenment, I remembered how more than once I thought I knew a subject, could have passed exams in it, then someone had come along and spoken on the same subject, and in a flash I had realised that never until that moment had I understood it. Whereupon the comment in wonder: So this *is* what it meant!

Much of which comes into focus in these words by Dr Suzuki: 'The living by Zen makes us aware of a mysterious something which escapes intellectual grasp.'

Apparently I had not got the 'something'. Accustomed as the Highland mind may be to apparitions, second sight, 'other' states of mind, even herons' legs –

And then in a flash it came: The 'something' was of the nature of the 'I' which I have tried to isolate in the opening paragraphs of this article. It was of that kind, in that realm of experience, and was lit by the same certainty. There is never any doubt when this happens, just as there is never any doubt of a taste in the mouth, or of a garden seen through a door that opens in a wall, or of a far country seen through a gap. That I should be here – in the country where the Eastern mind has been adventuring! It does not matter whether one can as yet see 'the way' or not, this is the country through which the way runs. Here is exploration in territory which our Western psychologies have either not seen or not understood.

But I had better forsake incoherency at this point, for the flash lit up such peculiar aspects of everything from literature to psychiatry's descriptions of delusions that I must leave an attempt at getting less lost to another article.

18

Eight Times Up

THE NEEDLE IN THE HAYSTACK has nothing on the self lost in 'incoherency', as my previous article attempted to indicate. Finding the self is as astonishing as finding the needle, and as rare. The quest in this region of the mind is comparable with the physicist's in his region of the infinitesimals, and the results as astonishing. I want to stress that this is a practical affair, where getting down to mind in one region is like getting down to earth in the other, and has to be so pursued. Only results matter. Admittedly the vague or 'mystical' will interfere however one tries to exclude them, for the quest is into the unknown or uncertain. A physicist at the extremity of his particular knowledge has been known to get a hunch. When pursuing his hunch he occasionally astonishes himself by discovering, say, X-rays. But he would not have made the discovery if he had not been, as the East has it, 'on the way'.

Long pursuit, sheer hard work, concentration, discipline, a hunch, and, with luck, an astonishment. That applies in both regions. And if an ordinary man were to indulge in the luxury of a hunch, en passant, it might take the mythical form of seeing both the investigators, in mind and matter, East and West, pursuing with comparable logics (psychological and mathematical) their individual ways, and finding themselves, as they went, Drawing nearer and nearer to each other until finally, in a flash, their ultimate findings coalesced. That would certainly settle Duality!

Is the myth too fantastic? Yet what is a myth but a hunch? If waves and particles are 'aspects' of an electron, what are mind and matter 'aspects' of? For the one thing that has been indubitably happening in science is that old absolutes – like Newton's space, time, matter, force – are being better under-stood as aspects of a four-dimensional continuum or other concept of a 'higher' reality. That appears to be the way things are going, whether we like it or not. And as atoms here seem to have more unchancy and fearsome attributes than any myths or fairy stories I know, let me get back to my simple concern with finding the self, that needle in the haystack.

Simple, but rare, very rare, this coming upon the self, as in that complex of the quiet evening and the fishing heron, which subsequently gave an insight into a Japanese painting and a poem. When we use the expression 'self-aware', we are not, I find in actual talk, being aware of the self in the way I mean. We can say 'self-aware' without at that moment being aware of the self at all. The use of this intellectual counter gives no guarantee that the user has ever experienced that awareness of himself with which I am here concerned. In fact the sound of words inhibits the evocation of the awareness and thus (as I in this instant discover) gives a pointer to the meaning or purpose of the Zen master's silence.

Let me try to get over this difficulty of communication by using the familiar pictorial device. Picture the person who has come upon that quiet evening scene and is involuntarily stopped in his tracks by the fishing heron. What happens inside his mind? A complete stoppage of all words, all thoughts. Even his breathing stops as though its physical action would interfere with an alertness that sustains itself in order to catch what is beyond hearing. Not with effort, but in pure wonder. A suspension of the whole being, body and mind, in a condition of wonder that has the feel of 'something' beyond the intellect which is magical. He gets this feel of himself, there. And this feel or consciousness takes as it were the shape of himself in the involuntary apprehension: That I should be here! The 'I' is like an apparition of himself, at once strange and familiar. In this sense it is objective, detached; though, more precisely, 'objective' and 'subjective' become two aspects of, in that moment, the abiding reality of the 'I'. To become self-aware in this way is, as far as I know, rare.

Yet what a jumble that last paragraph really is, difficult as it may have been to put together! Take the words 'stoppage of all words, all thoughts'. They have practically no meaning unless one has tried to stop them at some time or other. Try three o'clock in the morning, when a nagging worry prevents sleep. Attempt to stop the ceaseless flow of thoughts and observe what happens. One may succeed for five seconds the first time, but after that one gives up, the effort is too great. There is no controlling self, no will, to stop the idiotic flow. One gets into a complete subjective mess. Irritation may mount to fury, all to no purpose. The appalling cinema show goes on, and the only attendant consciousness is a humiliating recognition of one's utter automatic futility. Then contrast that state with the other and its abiding 'I'.

Or take that word 'magical'. Its imprecision is at once suspect. Did I use it as an anthropologist would, or a psychiatrist dealing with delusional states of mind, or a poet, or a writer of fairy tales, or as some elusive essence of them all? This is where one wishes semantics well! But the trouble with definition here is that by its very rigidity, its logical pattern, it must fail to confine what is illogical or irrational, like wonder.' One might as well try to define colour for a man born colour blind. Scientifically it can be defined for him with precision on the basis of different wave-lengths for different colours. And if the scientist could make him a gadget which measured the wave-lengths and recorded them in figures, the man could go about directing the gadget at things in a garden and with some assurance say 'red' of the poppies and 'green' of the cabbages, but of redness and greenness, not to mention their use in art, he would have no dimmest inkling.

Let me now try to give 'magical' its magical twist in the field of the heron (even if the field was the quiet bend of a river). For magic looks two ways; like any other emotional experience, it has its ambivalence, and this is of fundamental importance, as the psychologist knows. As whatever I say here will over-simplify, let me be as simple as possible and suggest that psycho-analytic probing into magic is concerned with the pathology of the human mind, with the mind that has lost its grip on reality and is taking refuge in retrogression to the primitive. Essentially the analysis deals with a process of mental disintegration. That is one way of looking at magic.

The other way is exactly opposed to that. Now the look is towards integration and the feeling of magical wholeness (as experienced in the field of the heron). And it is this aspect of the mind's two-way traffic, of ambivalence, that I find has been almost totally neglected by researchers into the human condition.

The literature on illness is immense, psychic, somatic, and psychosomatic. But of the opposite, of the human condition of wholeness, scarcely a word. It goes deeper than that. For example, listening-in to 'The Critics' one Sunday morning, I heard a male critic refer to a book as having a certain healthy quality, and immediately the female critic chimed in: 'Healthy! Oh, if you mean hygienic! ...' And there was a laugh. To speak of the healthy, in art, really! The male critic joined in the laugh. How clearly over the air came this modern instance of taboo!

But we know all about that, all about every kind of description and analysis of misery and destruction. We have had our noses continuously rubbed in it until the skin is gone. It is time we stopped having our noses rubbed for a while, artistically or brutally, brutally artistically or artistically brutally, primitively, apprehensively, analytically, fearfully, suggestively, totalitarianly, fantastically, monosyllabically, polysyllabically, unendingly, with dots or without, because our noses are sore. Destruction destroys. Soon there won't be a nose left to put our fingers to. When that happens, we're through. It's time we had a let-up on all this.

So back to the heron, the Godot that did at least turn up. Here was no destruction, no slightest apprehension of it. The very opposite. Not broken bits falling apart, but a calm cohering whole. Not fear but assurance. Not terror but delight. Not an internal subjective mess but an external objective scene, cool as the evening, held in a clarity that bathed the eyes and made them see as they had never seen.

This clarity is Wordsworth's light that never was on sea or land. Not any longer a vague light, but quite specifically this.

So with Keats 'magic casements'. This is the light in which they were seen. Some time or other – perhaps by a forlorn Highland sea-loch – Keats came upon himself as he stood and stared. When that happens one sees in a memorable way; that is, quite literally, in a way that memory cannot forget. What the imaginative faculty may do with the experience afterwards, in tranquillity, is a poet's business. Here the critic can only be speculative (as with the Highland sea-loch) and obscure, for the logical faculty is not the imaginative, but Keats is neither speculative nor obscure, he is precise and clear. And if I had to ask a question here, it would be the searching one: How is it that what was so memorable to Keats has also been so memorable to so many?

But if we must give speculation an innings, let it be with a writer like D. H. Lawrence, because he had more than his share of the restlessness of our age. Why so restless that he had to keep shifting from place to place? What was he hunting? Did he ever find it, and, if so, precisely when? In such biographies of him as I have read I can find no clear answers to my questions. Possibly to expect an answer may seem absurd, because we all know this vague restlessness only too well, and it bites none the less for being vague, even the more. One gets bitten by gnats in places one can't scratch.

Then I began to notice that when Lawrence had left behind his gnat-bitten self in, say, England, and come upon himself whole and fresh, in new territory, like Sicily, the restlessness vanished and he wrote divinely. It was as if this kind of environmental shock were needed to destroy the gnats, to let Lawrence emerge and find himself again, whole, among his trees and wild flowers, and in this way, in this light, to see the trees and wild flowers with such clarity, so magically, that he could use blue anemones to light the way even to hell, memorably.

In Dr. F. R. Leavis's book on Lawrence I found this quotation from *The Rainbow*: 'Self was a oneness with the infinite. To be oneself was a supreme gleaming triumph of infinity.'

Now the one thing Lawrence detested was conventional attitudes or modes that smothered the quick. That was death to him, and he warred against it, especially in sex, because here hypocrisy, social hypocrisy, seemed to him particularly virulent. But elsewhere, too, against all vague soul upliftings and such. It was from this context that the quotation stood out. Accordingly I had to assume that Lawrence in using these words was being as specific as he knew how about an actual experience; and when it comes to know-how in modern writing I cannot readily think of a better craftsman. So I had to put it to myself as impersonally as possible: when Lawrence found this 'Self' that was at one with the infinite, was it the self, the 'I', which I am concerned with here – and concerned, may I say once more, not in any 'mystical' sense but as a matter of fact in actual living!

At least for Lawrence such moments would seem to have been as rare as I believe them to be. For normally it takes an emotional shock, environmental or other, to bring them into being. But the East has long known this, as Dr.. Suzuki makes plain: 'An intense emotional disturbance often awakens in us a mysterious power of which we have ordinarily been unaware.'

When Proust writes of the 'identity underlying all the works of a great writer; the comparisons of critics are of no interest compared with this secret beauty'. I seem to see, from the aesthetic angle, the underlying identity as the identity of the

104

self, the 'I' – I can think of no other underlying identity. And when I equate Proust's 'beauty' with Suzuki's 'mysterious power' I am conscious of trying to be as precise in this region as the physicist in his. 'Mysterious' may look like a vague or magical word. 'Mysterious power.' But power here is the equivalent of force in the region of matter, and force to the physicist is just as mysterious as power to Suzuki. What gravitational force is, or electrical force, or nuclear force, the physicist does not know. He knows them by what they do, and can calculate their doings with exactitude. He knows, for example, that this force falls off inversely as the square of the distance and so with confidence sends sputniks aloft. But what this enormously powerful gravitational force is, he does not know, and in his groping to find out he is not unlike primitive man taking a glance over his shoulder to surprise what cannot be seen. There is magic in both realms, mind and matter, and here the twin exploratory attempt to discover the laws by which magic works may result in a vast extension of human knowledge and understanding. May I be forgiven the involuntary reflection; how stupid, how dull, to blow man to bits as he stands on such a threshold!

And when I hold the reflection for a minute I hear Bertrand Russell remarking that man has a fifty-fifty chance of survival. An even chance that the bombs won't go off. A shade more optimistic, I put the favourable odds at eight to seven. But then, again, I am probably being influenced by this exploratory trip East. It is said of Bodhidharma that he sat so long in meditation that his legs fell off. Whereupon the Japanese made a legless doll so weighted inside that however you knocked it down it sat up again; and then made a popular song:

Such is life—

Seven times down,

Eight times up!

I hope to come up for a final round in the next article and, with help from fragments of a remarkable esoteric teaching, make a final effort to arrest and have a close look at this elusive T.

19

Landscape Inside

A NOVELIST CANNOT WRITE ABOUT people in a vacuum. They must have a background, and the background becomes part of them, conditioning to some extent almost everything they do. When this works at a fairly deep level, it can be quite unconscious. I can't remember (though I may be wrong) ever having described a Highland scene for the scene's sake. Always the scene had something to do with the mind of the character who found himself there. The difference here is like the difference between a colour photograph of a landscape and an artist's painting of it. In the painting, the artist, with his kind of mind, is present. In the colour photograph no mind is present. Perhaps this explains why so many set descriptions of scenes, like sunsets, can be boring or why lovely Highland glens, shot in colour film, have sometimes been dubbed picture-postcardy by critics. However, let me stick for a moment to the novelist, who does in fact often describe the mood of a character by describing the background, the physical scene. Or vice versa. There is a sort of oblique traffic between the two, and this can thicken the texture of both. When the character, for example, is on top of the world, the world becomes a wonderful place. When he is feeling depressed or nihilistic then the world around him becomes detached and uncaring. When one hears a critic describing the background as the principal character in a novel, it means that the background is actively directing the character. This can often happen in the Highlands.

Possibly it happens because of the powerful nature of the Highland scene: the mountains, the glens and straths, the moors, the features that never change?

Yes – and no. For there is really a continuous change going on in these physical features – or, at least, in the way they appear to the eye. This, of course, is due to the light which can change from minute to minute. It sometimes produces fantastic dramatic effects, not merely in colour but in bulk, in mass. On a hot summer day, for instance, the mountains lose height; they seem to flatten, to squat down, as Highland cattle do, or deer, or other brute beasts. Then the sky hazes over, the evening comes, and wisps of mist form here and there. If one of these wisps begins to tie itself round a mountain, the mountain slowly rears up and sticks its head in the sky. I remember once, in Glen Affric, we had been out on the hill all day, and when we got back I found myself standing at a front window of the lodge, looking down the loch. To the right, rising sheer from the loch, there is a row of mountains over three thousand feet. They were covered with snow, with black ridges or stripes here and there; in the fading light they now looked gigantic, fearsome, and I realised, as never before, how small would be the chances of survival of anyone caught there with the long night coming down. Even as I watched, outlines were being smothered.

Perhaps I may seem too concerned with the effect of background on the individual. But finally that is the only thing one can be sure about – the effect on oneself. Too much is generalised about the Highlands, so vague romantic notions are born, often sentimental, nostalgic. However, one knows what happens to oneself, and then one meets others and gets their experiences, and so one may with reasonable confidence go on to talk in a general way about the effect of the Highland background on the Highland people. Yet I must confess that I always feel happier when dealing with something specific. So let us take music – say, some of these haunting old Gaelic songs or melodies, the sort that can change a Highlander's mood in a moment in spite of him. In how many of them, especially from the Outer Isles, is the rhythm of the sea. How often through the centuries his folk listened to the wind on stormy nights, heard the tumult of the sea, the mounting tumult, the thunderous smash, the recession. Or had long thoughts on a summer's day as they looked down on cockle strands. Something of this comes into the music, so that a snatch of it, at any time, anywhere, will have its profound effect. It will bring him to himself, the essence of himself, however buried under social or other accretions. 'When I am with myself' is a literal translation of the title of one of these old songs. Yet from this individual experience to the general experience may be but a step – say, across a threshold into a genuine ceilidh. In this particular region of the mind, place and people meet. The outer and the inner landscapes merge.

Yet there is a difficulty here, for the general experience or ordinary ceilidh can on occasion, as I have hinted, generate the vague emotionalism that so readily spills over into sentimentality. This is the point where one could wish to be as precise as a mathematician. But one cannot have both the emotion and the mathematics? I wonder.

Some time ago I was invited to a dinner on top of the Outlook Tower in Edinburgh by a group, a club, of distinguished Edinburgh and Glasgow men, trying to prove that though East is East and West is West the twain can meet on occasion. By a happy chance, a regimental pipe band was heard on the Castle esplanade, so we all quite naturally trooped out from the claret to a high grandstand view of the pipe band going through its paces, beating retreat. A vague mist hung around the capital city, and the sun, low down, was a rich red, doing its best to look as if it had been painted by William McTaggart. And there, down there, were the pipes, with their music from the islands and the glens, from far off things long ago, from the Celtic mist or twilight. But when we really listened and looked what we actually saw were pipers and drummers going through their evolutions with absolute precision, like geometrical designs in fluid motion, as if the whole performance had been laid on by some ultimate mathematician. Yet the emotion was of the pride and the power and the glory.

From music to colour. And there is no need to despair at the mention of colour in the Highlands. Of course an ordinary writer can do nothing about it, except set down the simpler facts which he may have observed, as, for example, that the best time for colour is spring and autumn. In the height of summer the glens, the straths, are too uniformly green. And then a Czech film director and refugee, sweeping my seasons aside, said to me, 'No, no, no: if only we had a colour process for that.' Spring had not yet wakened, the mountain sides were withered, and a shafting sunlight played on the blaeberry bloom of the bare birches. The moment so seen by a stranger warms the inner landscape and is never forgotten.

Or, again, in Skye. Many years ago, I was staying in a small hotel at Carbost. The only other guest was Professor Collie of London University, the distinguished mountaineer, who charmed more than one evening with descriptions of climbs in the Himalayas, the Rockies, and elsewhere. His quiet precise manner gave an extraordinarily vivid verisimilitude to the solution of sudden rock-face problems of great difficulty and danger; in particular a certain feat of endurance can still haunt me. Once, when the talk must have veered to the local scene, he told me that the most memorable stretch of colour he had ever seen anywhere was on the moor in front of the Cuillin – on the Glenbrittle side, as you come up from Talisker. I had seen it the day before. Its tone was somewhere between amontillado and a medium or richer sherry, but it looked like an immense living golden hide. The wind rippled and played on it in a light-hearted frolic. The glow of life was there, as if the earth were a beast. Perhaps the earth has a life of its own. Every new physical fact discovered by the scientists is more astonishing than the last.

To see the Hebrides along the horizon on an opalescent evening; to look at your chart, at the small cross marking an unknown anchorage; to head towards an island that keeps its distance in the silence beyond the beat of the engines as the opalescence deepens.

But landscape is more than a matter of stringing beads. There is a way of looking at the simplest scene if it is to remain. An artist once told me that you must consider a bit of landscape three separate times before it really sticks in your memory. The first time you look at it very carefully, going from detail to detail, all round. Then you come back and take it in all over again. Then a third time. After that it remains with you. For in the ordinary course scenery is the vague sort of thing we rush through – like a conducted tour on television. Nothing much remains beyond a glorified blur. One has got to stop and look, be quite precise, factual. You can't stop the tele, of course, but you can draw up if you are in a motor car or on a motor bike or, better, on your own two feet. So when a scene surprises, stop and look at it with the artist's eye by way of experiment. After that you go on and, in the ordinary manner, forget all about it. But later – years afterwards perhaps – that scene will come back with an extraordinary clarity. Like a tune you had completely forgotten. But no tune will come back to you unless, when you first heard it, you made some effort to remember it.

I know that raises difficulties; for example, the value of a first impression; or, for that matter, impressionism in painting generally. But I think that we may take it that Cezanne looked at many apples, even more than three times, before he painted them in a memorable way.

However, there is something further here that I hesitate to mention because it is so elusive, so difficult to convey.

Have you ever, as a small boy, wandered farther from home than you meant to or were aware of – say, up a strath or valley – until you found yourself in a place where you had never been before? All at once you realise that you are in this strange place. Stock still, not breathing so that you can listen, you stare at grey rocks with whorls of lichen on them like faces, tree-roots like snakes, the trees themselves heavy with leaves and silent. Your heart comes into your throat. Quietly, very quietly, you get back onto the path, then take to your toes for all you are worth. This may have been the first experience of panic fear – the first meeting with the old Greek god. But you also met someone else there, much nearer to you than Pan: you met yourself.

There is no esoteric or hidden meaning here. I am trying to be quite factual; simply saying that unless you come upon yourself in some such way, as an element present in the scene or landscape, the chances are that you will forget it, however long you look at it. And I suspect that the artist's exercise of looking three separate times was not only to observe the detail, which is essential, but to give this special kind of awareness a chance to happen. It can be magical and memorable when it does, and only when it does.

20
Highland Space

THERE IS THE STORY OF the man who after the last war (he had done most of his fighting in the desert) came back to his home, a croft between mountains, and stood the austere scenery for three days and nights, and then beat it. The mountains had got on top of him, the silence, the loneliness. I was told the story at the point where he was passing through Inverness on his way south. Apparently he had no definite destination. He was a piper, too.

Experience on that level, at that pitch of intensity, can be understood only by those who have had something like it. There are lower levels, as in the case of the two ladies to whom I had suggested a three-day motoring tour of the Western Highlands by way of brief introduction to that inexhaustible variety of land and sea. They cut the tour short, one saying to the other, 'When you have seen one glen you have seen the lot,' and returned to their native city.

Not to mention those who exclaim, 'Ah, how lucky you are, living in the remote and beautiful Highlands!' when you know that after one tough-weathered week there, with 'nowhere to go', they might have their first dim notion of what troubled the piper. In comparison, there is innocence in the face with the considering eyes and the mouth that asks on its own, 'Do you mean to say you stay here all the year round?'

But however the instances be added, what is fundamental in the lot is the fear of empty space; at first, fear of the 'vacant' places, brooding mountains, sterile distances; and then of the appalling outward swoop into space itself, into infinite emptiness, into Pascal's horror of it, the *horror* vacui. So fundamental does this seem that one takes it as a permanent, if submerged, element in our mental make-up, in what we call human nature. Certainly some of the first English poets to visit the Highlands were afflicted in this way.

But is this experience in fact universal; is it really an invariable psycho-logical ingredient, a constant, in the nature of the human animal? Or are we up to the old game of equating human nature with our particular culture pattern? This is the kind of question that sent Jung, I understand, to foreign places and other culture patterns, so that he might look back at the one he had left. When this is done, astonishing things can happen.

My own particular astonishment came from looking at some Oriental pictures, and, in particular, reproductions of the works of Sesshu recently published in Japan. It is one of those luxurious editions of the works of an old master, but as I turned over the pages I became disturbed by an element other than the novelty or strangeness of what was portrayed, by an element that wasn't as it were in the picture at all but yet was there – if only I could uncover it. To take a simple example, with the translated title, 'Plumtree'. It is a vertical picture or hanging scroll, painted in ink on paper. The limb of an old plum tree comes out from the right of the picture about halfway up and disposes a broken, mis-shapen branch and a couple of long slender stems on the air. This, of course, is exquisitely done; but, still this was not all – and then suddenly I realised that what 'made' the picture was the unpainted surface, the empty air. At such a moment both the picture and the mind are lit up; all is included and questioning vanishes.

To take a more complex example of natural scenery, described simply as 'splashed-ink landscape', and completed by Sesshu in 1495 at the age of seventy-six. I feel sure a lot has been written about this picture, and indeed the considerable amount of pictographic writing at the top of the scroll was added, I gather, by other hands. However, the only point in my writing here is to try to show the effect of the picture on one completely ignorant of pictographs and informed native criticism, if not without some response to the natural scene. My concern is with space.

The eye, then, is caught immediately by a tree in the foreground, and behind it – or, more exactly, above it – the looming shapes of two mountain peaks. These three objects are discontinuous; they are not linked together in the perspective with which the Western eye is familiar, so familiar that its absence instantly conveys a sense of bewilderment… Then within the bewilderment came the uncanny feeling that these vague peaks were not simply apart in space but were being actively created by space. They were being born out of it. Space was the creative source.

But there was more than that – though now I hesitate, for, when the eye looks steadily, an odd, perhaps entirely personal, illusion can arise; in this case it was the illusion of movement, of, as I have suggested, active creation. To compare broadly: whereas in a Western painting the moment is arrested, static, here the moment is caught from what has been described as the eternal flux of becoming and unbecoming. I know this has inexhaustible philosophic implications, but I am not concerned with these at this point, only with seeing and experiencing. Just as I once saw the dawn coming out of space on the mountains above Lochbroom. The curve of the mountains took the light in a way which made me realise that the earth was a great ball turning in space. Dawn was not entirely the rosy-fingered affair of our traditional poetry. Nor, for that matter, did the rosy fingers thereafter lose their appeal or our human condition its interest; quite the contrary: because of that which had been added.

As for the third – or at least now the fourth – element in the picture, the splashed-in tree, it was no longer 'the tree' so much as 'tree'. Nor was this quite the platonic notion of the ideal tree. Somewhere I have read that Sesshu got the splashed effect of the foliage by taking a little bunch of straw, dipping it in the ink, and then dabbing it on the paper. Which may permit the reflection that American action painting is neither so new nor so revolutionary as has been bruited; and the further reflection that in Sesshu's case this irruption of the irrational is not the whole picture. These old masters had a way of putting things in their place.

One more picture by Sesshu I should like to mention, though it is not included in the de luxe volume. It is called 'Seven Sages in a Bamboo Grove'. Why such a title should warm the human breast I hardly know. Perhaps it is not so much what they might say or do as that they should be there saying and doing it. Anyway, tradition has it that the seven met in the bamboo grove and gave themselves to painting pictures, making poems and playing music – having, of course, already attained freedom from the clogging absurdities of all negative and destructive emotions. But what particularly struck me was a final remark by the Japanese critic to the effect that such a picture could be painted only by one who had himself attained the mind which would adorn the bamboo grove.

And that is the mind that brings us back to space. Many of those old master painters in Japan were, like Sesshu, Zen priests. Zen is a sect of Buddhism and enough is being written about it in the world today to make it unnecessary for me to say how little I know about it. Not that knowing, I find, or learning or even deep study helps much, for the central experience of enlightenment (revelation is, perhaps, our word) can come only when thinking or the logical processes stop. That is not to decry thought, of course; merely to make it clear that enlightenment is not an end product of thought. However, the one thing I wish to avoid is verbal entanglement, so let me say briefly, then, that apparently our fear of space, the *horror* vacui, is not a fear or horror for all mortals. Certainly it is not a fear in Zen, which uses words like Emptiness, Nothing, the Void, quite commonly, but always in the paradoxical sense that Emptiness is not emptiness, space is not Void, yet, again, that they are these in the moment before they are not. To take the further step and hold these ultimate opposites in unity may be a true experience, but if so its expression – the communication of such a state of being – can never be more than a hint by the use of paradox. At this point the interesting thing about Sesshu's landscape is that in it you see him resolving the paradox. He paints his picture (in the bamboo grove, I hope) and the eye sees his space or Void, the plenitude of his Nothing.

But let me quote a verse from a living Scottish poet to help me out. It might have been written on a famous Zen anecdote concerning the master who referred to a flock of wild geese. 'But, Master,' replied his pupil, 'they have already flown away.' The master administered a physical shock (sure way of stopping logical processes) and the pupil, instantly experiencing the enlightenment he had so long and painfully sought, saw that though the geese had flown away, they had not flown away. Here is the verse from the poem 'Advices of Time' in Norman MacCaig's recently published book, *A Common Grace:*

The bird flies in the mind, and more than bird:
Times dies somewhere between it and its flight.
The bird flies in the mind, and more than mind:
Sunsets and winds and roofs enrich the light
That makes it bird and more than bird, till they
Can never fly away.

I am not suggesting that this is a description of the enlightenment (satori) that comes through Zen. But clearly it is 'on the way' – the opposite way to what the piper took, when he beat it from the looming mountains, or from some childhood fear of vacant places, loneliness, the dark.

21

Remember Yourself

OCCASIONALLY AN EXPERIENCE THAT SEEMS personal and unique is discovered to be neither. The moment of this discovery is always delightful. I mentioned fragments of an esoteric teaching at the end of my last article because in them I found an effort to isolate that very 'I' which I had been concerned to arrest and make real, the 'I' that is so rare an evocation of the self that it turns even the moment's environment magical.

Now I had gone what seemed to me a considerable distance in my investigation of the nature of this experience, far enough to check it against the actual experiences of other ordinary folk who had no knowledge of mystical or esoteric religions or literatures. In at least three instances I found the intensity of their experience far beyond what I have tried to evoke or communicate in the simple incident of the heron. I cannot truthfully say that they were far beyond anything of the kind I had ever experienced myself because if they had been I should not have been able to appreciate them. Here it is almost a law that one cannot see or appreciate beyond one's own level of being and cannot communicate except to those on at least a similar level. I say 'almost' because it is not quite; despite certain Eastern teachings, not in my experience. However, that is a refinement or distinction of no particular significance at the moment. The extraordinary thing to me was that the importance of the experience did not seem to be recognised by our philosophies or psychologists, yet the more I tried to grasp its nature in a realistic way the more important it became.

Then I happened on a book called *In Search of the Miraculous* by P D Ouspensky. Its subtitle runs, *Fragments of an Unknown Teaching.* The teacher of the fragments was Georges Gurdjieff whom Ouspensky met in Moscow in 1915. The book describes the meeting, and what it led to, in the interesting human way that one may encounter in a good novel. Finally a group or 'school' was formed and Ouspensky, as one of the group, recorded Gurdjieff's teaching.

Now manifestly Ouspensky was not only a brilliant linguist but also deeply versed in our Western philosophies and sciences, with a particular flair for logic and mathematics. I had not – and have not yet – read his books which have a slant, in particular, I gather, on the 'mathematicalness' of everything in the world. I can only speak out of impressions gained from reading the 'miraculous' book, and when he went East in search of this miraculous I envisaged him as I might a mathematical physicist in search of some equation that would resolve apparent opposites or contradictions, that would turn as it were old 'absolutes' into new 'aspects' of a higher or more inclusive reality. 'There is a dark inscrutable workmanship that reconciles discordant elements,' says Wordsworth with a poet's assurance. Ouspensky had obviously some such hunch, and his equipment was not only impressive but, for such as myself, reassuring.

His search for the 'esoteric schools' of the East failed, but in Gurdjieff he found enough fragments of their 'unknown' teaching to keep him busy for the rest of his life.

Gurdjieff, as seen through Ouspensky's eyes, is a much more elusive character. He has been seen through other eyes, and a considerable literature has grown up about him, and particularly about an establishment he set up and ran for a time near Fontainebleau in France. But I know little or nothing of this and I am concerned here only with one quite precise personal experience (as indicated in the heron incident) and what I am searching for now is some verification of it from outside, some external estimate of its validity and, if possible, its significance or importance.

Accordingly I make no reference to the extraordinary range of Gurdjieff's teaching; to its astonishing if not fantastic cosmology, for example. Yet for my purpose, one or two cardinal points should be made; and, first, that only a normal man can benefit from the teaching. The abnormal, the obsessed, the pathological are excluded. Why this is so is made quite clear. Secondly, the basis of the whole teaching is material, but materiality is the noun used, not materialism. Just as matter is ultimately an affair of 'vibrations' to the physicist, so is mind also to Gurdjieff, who talks of 'vibrations' (manifestations of energy) much as our scientists do. When this seemed too material by half at a first glance, I had to grope around for some handhold or other, and as vibrations suggested music, I had to realise that basically music is a matter of vibrations. Getting all the implications here was as hard work as learning to play the violin. From vibrations to the profound experience of great music – but I must leave it there, trusting that I have at least been able to indicate the context out of which one day Gurdjieff asked the members of his group what it was in his teaching that had so far impressed them, or, as he put it. 'What is the most important thing that we notice during self-observation?'

They all had a shot at answering, but Gurdjieff was dissatisfied. 'Not one of you noticed,' he said, 'that you *do not remember yourselves*. You do not feel *yourselves* … you are not conscious of *yourselves* … Only those results will have any value that are accompanied by self-remembering. Otherwise you yourselves do not exist in your observations. In which case what are all your observations worth?'

That flummoxed them. And, later, he rubbed it in: 'If you ask a man whether he can remember himself, he will of course answer that he can. If you tell him that he cannot remember himself, he will either be angry with you, or think you an utter fool.'

So Ouspensky really got going on this difficult exercise of self-remembering and in time became convinced that 'I was faced with an *entirely new problem which science and philosophy had not, so far, come across.'* The italics are his and conveyed to me something of the astonishment and revelation by which he was struck.

Struck myself – as I was – I might have left it there. But not so Ouspensky. Whenever Ouspensky is struck he flies to mathematics and draws a diagram. In this case he drew an arrow, a fine long arrow, with the barbed end pointing at 'the observed phenomenon', and of course away from himself. But now if he were going to remember himself at the same time as he was observing the phenomenon, he would also have to have the arrow pointing at himself. So he put a barb on the other end, the end towards himself. Now the arrow was barbed at both ends; was directed simultaneously both at the observed phenomenon and at himself. In brief, he had to be conscious both of object and subject at the same time. Somehow or other there had to be a 'self' present that was aware of this difficult operation and succeeded in observing it.

Anyone may test the difficulty for himself, but if he can for an instant catch a glimpse of this 'self', he will find that the experience has quite a different feel or taste from that which arises in the ordinary way when he uses the expression 'conscious self'. Anyway, this is what Ouspensky found; and found also that the experience is very rare and of such importance that, as we have seen, it drove him to italics.

Now all this seemed so near my heron experience, if I may so call it, that I began to feel 'warm'. But I could not be certain because of two differences: in the first place, my experience had not only been not difficult but quite involuntary, and, in the second, memory or 'remembering' had had nothing to do with it. Far from 'remembering myself', or remembering this aspect of the self (the 'I'), I had come upon it with surprise. In fact when I had described at length a similar boyhood experience in a book I had used the expression 'come upon myself'. But perhaps I have already made this distinction clear enough.

So here I was with a nice piece of detection on hand, prepared to follow Ouspensky through every twist of his hunt at trying to grasp this elusive affair. The 'involuntary' difference was soon disposed of, because Ouspensky discovered, when he thought back into his childhood, that he had had this experience quite involuntarily. Again he makes it clear that he had subsequently come upon it in a dramatic change of environment, with the involuntary comment: 'That I should be here!'

So far so good. But what of the 'remembering' element? and, after all, 'self-remembering' was Gurdjieff's term, and as his psychological analysis is to me of an unequalled clarity, I might have to give his term a technical status. Nowhere does Ouspensky in his book or Gurdjieff in his teaching specifically exclude the 'remembering' element, or at least what the word 'remembering' means to me.

Now all this may seem at first contact a small terminological wrangle about what doesn't fundamentally matter anyhow, but clearly to Ouspensky self-remembering held a profound significance which our science and philosophy had missed. I can see him laying hold of it as a physicist might some new element or particle among the infinitesimals. And as for Gurdjieff – it meant nothing less than that only at the moment of self-remembering is a man conscious. Now if his self-remembering was the same as my 'coming upon myself', then I could gather what he meant when he went on to say that at all other moments man is not conscious of himself. So he differentiates man conscious from man unconscious. Unconscious man is mechanical man, a piece of mechanism to which things happen. Conscious man is the man who has come upon his own self, the 'I', the conscious self that can take control and master mechanical happenings. This realisation is the first step on the way to levels or dimensions of being with which his teaching is concerned.

As I read, it began to dawn on me that perhaps Gurdjieff meant that what had been rare and involuntary to me and to others should not – and need not – be so. It could be cultivated. One must make an effort every now and then to isolate the self or 'I', to remember to do it, to self-remember. Self-remembering could be his expression for this conscious effort.

But to bring my attempt at detection to a finish, let me refer to a volume by Ouspensky called *The Fourth Way*, published in 1957, posthumously published, for both Gurdjieff and Ouspensky are dead. It consists mostly of 'verbatim extracts' from talks given by Ouspensky, and his answers to questions, over a number of years. Here at last is his answer to a direct question on the meaning of self-remembering: 'Self-remembering is not really connected with memory: it is simply an expression. It means self-awareness, or self-consciousness. One must be conscious of oneself. It begins with the mental process of trying to remember oneself …'

As an assessment of the heron experience from outside, this seemed good enough to me. Whether evoked involuntarily or voluntarily, by chance or by deliberate 'remembering', the 'I' was apparently one and the same.

The Taste

As I look over the articles in this series now concluding I wonder if, finally, it would be possible to give a working name to the 'mysterious something' which escapes intellectual grasp, as Suzuki put it, but which the 'I' experiences. Can it be brought down from something like transcendence onto the practical level of living?

Certainly this 'something' usually remains hidden in all kinds of learned discussion or esoteric teaching, so hidden that it does not seem to be there. Consider disquisitions on ethics, theology, aesthetics, etc. Listen to the voice intoning or thundering from a pulpit. Or to the calm voice of the botanist relating the life history of a strawberry and then to the chemist's voice in a detailed analysis of the berry. Or even to my own voice on the growing of strawberries, for I grow a lot of them. At this moment I am resting a broken back from a bout on the strawberry bed. What final knowledge, then what ultimate something, do I get from my arduous cultivation of the berry?

Its taste.

If its taste were not delightful would I pursue it through sweat to a broken back, would I remorselessly hunt the underground infiltrations of bishop-weed (how did it get that name?) or couch grass? And if a psychiatrist, who knows about couches, began to explain that such weeds led an underground life of virulent and unkillable strength and that every here and there, unpredictably, they sent up visible shoots to throttle the berry, what would I answer? I would answer, You're telling me! If the bishops and psychiatrists got into a high falutin' wrangle about all this, enough to fill tomes of surpassing subtlety, what would they forget? The taste of the berry.

To me this is not fanciful, it is the one thing I know. Here the 'something' is for me as real as the berry. This, as far as I am concerned, is what the berry is for. But I do not expect the berry in some 'mystical' fashion to fall into my mouth. Work and sweat and, unless I have grown cunning about it, lumbago. If there isn't the taste, the rest is sweat for nothing. Meaningless. The taste is the meaning. But surely there is some high and wonderful meaning beyond this, surely if . . .? A Zen master would politely wait until you had woven your metaphysical yarn into its most distinguished pattern and then, according to Dr Suzuki, reply: 'I think it is going to rain'. Strawberries need a fair amount of rain. Then you have strawberries and cream.

Now, words convoluting in thin air may lead to an ultimate concept like Enlightenment, as the East has made plain. But does such a concept have a taste? Back to mind comes the Zen master and for him at least I am convinced it has. That's why his eyes, to use Yeats's word, are 'gay'. He knows the taste of Enlightenment as a simple gardener the taste of a berry. In the Zen region, so to speak, if strawberries are not about they are in the offing. Here the very pulse of life is spontaneous, not laboured, not solemnly 'mystical'.

When a writer imagines he clearly understands something which he would like to communicate, then for him clarity is all and obscurity the enemy. That is why, I suspect, I have been wrapping 'mystical' in inverted commas. So let me have a closer look at the word and its everyday use.

Normally it has human connotations of vagueness, obscurity, and the general reaction is to shrug it off with the expression 'poor fellow' as one might in the case of a drunk who had achieved inarticulation. Gone all mystical, poor chap!

The involuntary picture of the fellow has usually an Indian background, where the sun reduces clothing to a loincloth respectable yet small enough to permit contemplation-of the navel. If the fellow lives in our climate, with topcoat and a muffler, the only decent thing a friend can do is, as delicately as possible, to direct him to a psychiatrist, who may discover retrogression to a childhood dependence on the mother, or even to the pre-natal womb-like security. From life's stormy seas, this is his unconscious method of escape. Nirvanic: back to Nirvana. West or East, topcoat or loincloth, the same thing.

Now what always bothered me here was getting a grip on any reality behind 'mystical', getting the taste. of the mystical performance. For I had to assume to begin with that the Indian mind had been trying to cultivate its berry. For me to repeat a word like Nirvana and then think I understand all about it is too childish, especially when I know that the East can make metaphysical rings round me with the greatest ease. If a Harley Street psychiatrist, with his penetrating knowledge of mental regression, were to impute some such condition to a Zen master, the master might suggest that the psychiatrist should take up golf, and, when he could go round St Andrews in 67, come back and they might have a little talk. For many of these Zen masters are also masters of the arrow and the sword.

In the usual solemn 'mystical' regions, however, all seems to be struggle and sweat, with not a glimpse of strawberries in an offing howsoever remote. That is my difficulty with 'mystical', and manifestly the difficulty of others, too. For where does the road run from here, towards what, if any, unimaginable berries? Of an answer to that practical question not a practical word.

Not even by Gurdjieff and Ouspensky. And when it comes to orthodox Buddhism it seems worse. Not a suggestion of human delight anywhere, not a taste.

I am far from being irreverent. If my loincloth knows anything at this verbal moment, it is sweat. Words are scrub and cacti in an all but impenetrable wadi. If, for anthological relief and variety, I look up Mr. Aldous Huxley's *Perennial Philosophy*, I may vaguely find myself on the 'divine Ground', but of a strawberry bed do I catch a beckoning glimpse? It cannot be altogether a deficiency in my vision that makes me think Mr. Huxley is not very good at strawberries because what I do see is his beckoning on, on towards regions of the four Noble Truths and the Eightfold Path.

Very well. Once again I will dive into these Truths.

It is unnecessary for me to say now that far from being knowledgeable here I am but a lost traveller, the ordinary man who doesn't know where he is, as he gazes at what is around him. But I submit that the theologians or esoterics (or even Mr. Huxley, whom I deeply respect) should not jump on me for that. If this is their territory, why haven't they put up signposts? If I saw a signpost with the inscription. 'To the Strawberry Bed – Third Wadi on the left.' I might have some notion of where I was.

So here's for the Truths and the Path as signposts! …

After an hour I surfaced with the bewildered feeling that I had been all wrong, that I had been lost in the wilderness, crying like a child for straw-berries, whereas what I should have been concerned to do in this enigmatic desert of pain and suffering, what I should have strenuously striven to do, was kill my craving for strawberries.

But of course. I should have remembered. I had been there before.

So where am I now in this hunt of mine? Back, doggedly back, to the heron's legs, hanging on by the skin of them to the intimation of a strange delight, of an 'I' that came upon itself there and knew that the created moment was good. And of a smile, too, beyond the blundering questions and the solemn words; a smile that comes on its own like a silent strawberry flower on the air.

As I write this I am surrounded by some acres of birches newly fledged, translucent in a green sunlight, and as I pause to listen critically to the singing of the birds I have to admit that they cannot go wrong. With them, I suppose, it is involuntary.

So one last effort at the voluntary, at the subdual of what Gurdjieff calls 'the negative emotions' and the Eightfold teaching calls our cravings.

But yet, and once more, for what? Where, where is the hidden berry, the *taste* that gives delight? Can it be that the ultimate berry here is some form of immortality? But what I am concerned about to the point of sweat and lumbago is the here and now, the living now. Eternity is irrelevant, and those who ask questions about it are futuristic and beside the point. However, in a last desperate sally, I return to the strenuous teachings – and discover, in a strange suspension of all thought, that when Buddha was questioned about the eternity of the universe and existence after death, he refused to answer. What did he do? According to the paintings and the statues, he smiled.

Then, as if the taste of some real berry were still in his mouth, he said: 'May every living thing be full of bliss.'

22

Light

Remember you quoted George Fox about there being only one light and so on, and I said I'd like to enquire further into the possible nature of his light and of other lights too, for the lights in one sense are one light and in another sense they're different? George Fox's light had for me a sort of Sabbath quietness in which all is seen and remembered in tranquility – without invoking Wordsworth. For that matter perhaps Wordsworth had his own variety of Fox's light – of the same family of lights, anyhow, as one member of a family is different from another.

But don't let me begin with such refinements. All I want to emphasise is the difference in the intensity of light. My variety of light is a light of wonder, of gaiety, of laughter, that is so marvellous that all ordinary things are born afresh, both on the face of the earth and inside the human noddle. That exaggerates, of course, what glimpses of light I may have had, but at least it suggests a distinction between the quiet, still light of an ethical acceptance and the vivid, flashing light of livingness, the extra intensity that irradiates life and being, that indeed seems to bring life to being for the first time.

Some Easterns speak of being 'born again' – *that* degree of intensity. But of course you know about this, and about Zen and koans and other paradoxical absurdities of the kind. You can see the young disciple of the relentless master sweating blood trying to find a rational meaning or explanation of the koan: day

---

Note. The basis of this article was recorded on tape for a friend and this accounts for its conversational tone.

after day he returns to the master's study, but before he has opened his mouth the master sees that he has failed, and waves him away. Then one day he comes, his face lit up, hardly able to speak, and the master sees that at last he has achieved enlightenment and welcomes him in. This enlightenment had come in an instant, a flash, like a flash of lightning.

But in this matter we need not stick to Zen. About the earliest lithograph I remember seeing was one portraying a shaft of light hitting Saul – who became St. Paul – on the road to Damascus. Saul was enlightened, or born again, as the Biblical record makes clear, so in all cases we have the ordinary sunlight of every day, then the shaft of lightning in which the spiritual life is born.

So much by way of preamble to what I came across in *The Scotsman,* so tucked away in the many pages that I missed it on a first scan through. Then purely by chance I came upon it and was so struck by astonishment that for a few moments I could hardly realise where or what I was. But I want to tell you as simply as I can what I read in *The Scotsman.* I'll read the main bits from the paper and join them up as I go along.

The heading reads, "U.S. scientists believe life may exist on Jupiter." The report goes on: "Life may exist on Jupiter according to two National Aeronautics and Space Administration scientists. This suggestion will put the kind of spotlight on Jupiter that used to be reserved for Mars and Venus. Once thought to be too cold and hostile to support life, Jupiter might now become the main point of interest of scientists. In a recent report the scientists told of experiments in which they duplicated Jupiter's atmosphere, then subjected it to a continuous barrage of man-made lightning, on the grounds that lightning, with sunlight, originally extracted life from Earth's primitive atmosphere. The chief of the Chemical Evolution branch of the Research Centre in California said the lightning barrage produced a variety of organic chemicals which he described as the 'forerunners of life' as it is known on Earth. No fewer than nine amino-acids were produced by the lightning, which he said was probably the most common form of energy on Earth before the appearance of life. Not only are amino acids the very building blocks of proteins, they also are the forerunners of the living cell's nucleus, D.N.A. 'Evidence suggests,' he went on to say, 'that Jupiter has the same building blocks of life that existed on Earth 4,500 million years ago when Earth probably had an atmosphere similar to that of Jupiter today."

I hope you have been struck by the remarkable parallelism between the birth of what we may call physical life on earth and the birth of what I have already called spiritual life. And when I said I was astonished and hardly knew where I was, I was no doubt exaggerating and yet, for instance, had the sensation of vast sweeping dimensions of space and time in which something central to the universe was being glimpsed – air, sunlight, lightning and the birth of life. Then, thousands of millions of years later, the same again. But now, in a psychic sense, the birth of the spirit. Dim apprehensions in which words like 'meaning', 'purpose' simply have no place – indeed, I feel fairly sure that in the aftermath of the lightning they continue to have no place, for the state of being achieved will be itself the meaning and the purpose.

Some such dim apprehensions I had when I wrote in *The Atom of Delight of* my assurance that life existed on other planets. But all this is too big for me just yet. I cannot really bring myself to think about it. It would require too much energy; I haven't got it. I've got to go into a meditation on it, I'm afraid; and at the very thought my mind baulks, probably because it knows it would only be floored and flounder. But that's not right either, because in the process of meditation, if one sank deeply enough into it, there might be glimpses – even flashes – of light, a little more intense, indeed more 'other' than the ordinary sunlight, beautiful as the ordinary sunlight is. But I have the feeling that the more of these moments, of these rare flashes, the more likelihood there is of the full lightning-flash itself.

However, I'm beginning to be critical, and want to be precise; for example, that word 'meditation' – what did I mean by it? Had it a precise, definite meaning or does it mean a sort of vague sinking into a warm, half-hopeful nothingness? The answer is precise and definite. The word 'meditation' implies two other words, one forrard and the other after it, namely 'concentration' and 'contemplation'. In the yoga sutras dealing with the training and use of the mind these three are clearly defined stages. Concentration is the simple act of fixing the mind's total attention on a particular thing or idea, like a flower or a donkey or a religious concept. I possessed a book on concentration and I remember one experiment from it. It was that I had to take my watch, look at the second hand as it went round and, looking at the second hand, not have any thought in my mind at all. I was surprised when I was told that if one could do that for forty seconds it would be quite remarkable. Well, I did it for just about forty seconds: and it took me several days before I was fairly sure that I had managed two minutes without any kind of thought entering my head. It's only then, in a trial like that, that you realise that this stream of consciousness, which people have written about and which Joyce used, is so continuous a stream, running *always* through the mind.

However, before we go on to meditation I would like to suggest that even concentration alone – that is the concentration of your mind entirely on the subject or object – can itself provide moments of delight. I remember once when I was sitting just as I'm sitting now in my chair looking out at the heather and things in the rockery that I saw some purple crocuses. One was a pretty big chap, and I went and had a look at him – looked inside – till the purple glowed; then I noted the lines inside, the shape of the whole, until I got the idea that I must now try so to fix details and shape that afterwards at any time I could remember the vivid whole. Well, I wasn't very good at remembering – when you try to concentrate on a particular thing, to fix it visually, you may find it has a habit of slipping from side to side – so the following day I went back and had a look again at the flower, and by the third time I really had got it in my mind, but particularly the purple colour that I'd never forget.

I've been reading a little book called *Zen Flesh and Zen Bones*. To begin with there are 101 short stories: and towards the end a sequence of 112 numbered paragraphs, each consisting of about a sentence or two, and described as 'the 112 ways to open the invisible door of consciousness,' which 'Shiva first chanted to his consort Devi, in a language of love we have yet to learn'. Well, here's one of them which, in passing, has to do with concentration;

'Look lovingly on some object. Do not go on to another object. Here in the middle of this object, the *blessing.*'

Assuming, then, you go out and find a blossom, then examine it as I suggested, on the lines that I did the crocus. Well, look at all the characteristics: first here's the flower. You concentrate on the flower. It's easy to concentrate in the particular instance because you've got to notice all the varied aspects of the flower – the colour, the light, stamens, pistil: each thing you go over, looking carefully, until at last it seems you really have every characteristic of the flower in your mind. Then still keep at it just to make sure you have got it all, including what you may have heard or read about it, everything. If your flower happens to be a cluster of blossom on a wild cherry tree, have a look at the total tree, and so take the flower itself within the tree background. Now what I want to point out is: it's easier to keep concentration going when you can follow it up by not only noticing the particular characteristics but also by writing them down. Well, when doing all that you would be engaged in an act of meditation. Meditation in the old yoga sense isn't something that's vague and elusive: it's a completely factual business.

There's a haiku – by Basho the poet – and he's thinking of his old friend. It goes;

> 'Our two lives.
>
> Between these
>
> Is the life of the cherry blossom.'

All this gives some notion of what I mean by concentration and meditation, and of how concentration has passed on to become part of meditation until the whole mind is engaged and no vagrant thought or mood can intrude.

But it's the next and final step that's the difficult one – and really quite impossible to describe because of its unique nature. So let me revert for a moment to that last stage in a meditation when you find yourself, after minutes, unable to produce one more thought. In the end thought itself gets choked and the mind becomes a void. It's at this point that the miracle happens, and the void, the void itself, gets lit up: the light spreads, burgeons; it is suffused with wonder, delight, a miraculous sense of freedom. And then you become aware of your self there, aware of a rare self, the self that interpenetrates all, sees and knows with a final certainty. I know some such self has been spelt with a capital S, just as the word certainty has been called Truth or Reality. But I don't want in this practical exercise to use capitals, or words like Mysticism, Transcendence and so on. There is no need, only a little application, persistence; failure and more persistence. The way is open. But one must go along it far enough for thought to get blocked and the void of no-thought to open out, for only then can enlightenment come.

The Ultimate, Unity, the One; I would suggest that such terms be avoided: they merely cloud with vagueness the processes of the exercise we are considering. If, however, during such exercise we get struck by a wayward gleam of light, by an intuition, we may find ourselves following it with extreme interest, the exercise forgotten. For example, when I used the word 'void' a few moments ago to describe the condition that follows the blocking of thought my mind made a jump or its own to the Eastern philosophic concept of the *Void*, which I had encountered in my reading but had been able to make little or nothing of. Then I remembered alternatives; *Emptiness, Nothing, No-thing.* Altogether they had described for me a final condition of being that seemed complete negation: certainly the opposite of anything paradisal in our sense. If Nirvana was nothingness, that was that. But the Void as a suspended condition, awaiting the light, illumination. This was something new for as the mind groped about for a new grip, it found another void, which had on occasion held it spellbound – the interval of silence, of no-sound, that follows a superbly played masterpiece. The mind does not remember a theme, a note: it lives and has its utmost being in the silence which contains the creative essence of the masterpiece and the creative essence out of which the masterpiece was composed. This luminous void is featureless, contains no-thing. (With luck, that is, for normally the silence is torn to shreds by frenetic applause before the last note has even had time to die decently.)

Happenings by the way, insights; and from some happenings we come to with the feeling that we have been away somewhere, wandering, and we sigh over the lost wandering as we return to the task on hand. For there is no need to be always too rigid with the exercise. Indeed, after some practice we find ourselves able to concentrate fairly quickly and to take in the main lines of a meditation in a comprehensive sweep. For example, I remember very vividly, after having meditated a few times on the crocus, I remember becoming extremely fascinated by its purple walls or petals. The purple glowed so richly that the flower itself seemed to expand, or at least the limiting lines of the petals were caught into the glow. There was nothing abnormal about this; only that I was seeing it with a more vivid intensity than at any time before; before, as it were, I had looked and passed on, now I looked and held on.

When this happens the visual image is never forgotten. This is important for it has to do with memory and the kind of imprint that never fades. But to elaborate this would take too long, and its practical aspects and techniques can be discussed in a factual way at any time; for the moment the gleam of the purple crocus holds me and I experience a rare expectancy, for something has flashed into my mind and I have the feeling of knowing what's coming before I quite know it. It's a joyous feeling. Rich and absurd and delicious. I see an artist with his brush or his pen almost unable to control his excitement. But control is absolutely necessary and I must resist these vagrant images, which can so readily knock one off the meditative line (though, in passing, they may convey a richness of being, an impression of extraordinary creative complexity, beyond any analysis and all in a moment) and get back to my now undying crocus.

What had flashed into my mind was a glimpse of wild geese flying out of sight from a Zen koan. So I deliberately recall the koan and see a Zen master and his pupil watching the geese until at last the pupil says, 'The wild geese are gone'. At that the master gives the pupil's nose a hefty tweak and says, 'They are not gone'. Whereupon the pupil suddenly and overwhelmingly achieves *satori* (enlightenment).

When I first read that koan I thought it pretty far-fetched. I could see a certain confusion in the use of terms that wouldn't need much logic to comb out; but beyond that, what? Nothing, really; though the very lack of logic might be amusing in an absurd way. Still, this tweaking of the nose (and, far more often, a real wallop from the master's stick) went a bit too far to be comfortable. To be clubbed, even nose tweaked, into enlightenment seemed an oddish proceeding. So I left it at that.

But now – held again by the purple crocus – I am not so sure. Enriched by its gleam I experience once more the rare expectancy, the creative complexity. Supposing at such a moment a friend walking with me in the garden says 'The crocus is dead', I can hear myself reply, 'The crocus is not dead'. And as he regards me with something more than astonishment and says, 'But the time of the crocus is past', I reply, 'The time of the crocus is not past'. If at this point I tweaked his nose, what then? I can hear him sorrowfully telling a mutual friend that I had, he very much feared, gone finally crackers. Did I use words like rich, absurd, delicious? But that's not the small revealing point which I must pin down at once and it's this: the pupil being a pupil would have had quite a long experience of concentrating and meditating. I hadn't thought of that. If he hadn't had he wouldn't have been walking with the master. But he had never, poor fellow, at the utmost stretch got beyond thought. He would have been near it, very near it and now the total unexpectedness, the sheer astonishment, of the nasal tweak turned his mind blank, void – and into the void flashed the light, enlightenment, satori, and the geese became immortal.

But that's not an explanation of the koan. There are no explanations of koans (though I gather a book of them has been written). To analyse a koan would be like analysing a living cell: after the analysis the parts are all there, but life is gone. Logic is a marvellous tool, but its uses are limited. Thought is meditation's prime mover, but the movement is directed to an end or an ultimate beyond it. as the Arts make clear. Is it possible, for example, to understand the works of the famous French impressionist painters except as variations on – back to it again – the gleam in the crocus? Apples, sunflowers, landscapes: one gets the glow before the mind can imagine an individual picture. What they painted is what never dies. Yet the ingredients of our exercise are all there. The intellectual critic would refer to the concentration of the artist on his theme, possibly remark on an abnormal concentration; then pass on to the visual features, colour, tone, construction, balance or imbalance – until he had given everything, missing nothing, in this his particular meditation on the picture. In brief, he analyses and explains it all, concentrates and meditates, but fails to pierce beyond his thought to an apprehension of the *whole* picture, the glowing unity, glowing from the light that comes from the region beyond thought.

I have tried to hint at the rich if not inexhaustible complexity that can follow a simple meditative exercise on a crocus when lit up by an insight or two, and have refrained from reflections on subject and object, the knower and the known, and philosophic profundities of the kind. Beware of big words, abstract sounds, when you are concerned with evoking light and life and livingness; and particularly so when passing from a crocus to, say, a specific corrosive deadly tangle in human relations as a new subject for meditation. And let it be in fact a specific and personal tangle. An actual experience, felt on the quick and darkly tangled. In the brain. There's a point at which generalisation and pious exhortation are an insult and a bore.

In such a case concentration is no difficulty. The difficulty lies in concentrating on anything else. The same with meditation. Every aspect of the tangle is gone over and over obsessively. Excessive brooding generates fears and hatreds. The case I have in mind had to do with land ownership, rights, and stealthy encroachments on property and privacy. It grew intolerable, until the younger man, whose rights were being eroded, reached the point of desperation when he discovered one morning that some of his ground beside a lawn had been ploughed up by the enemy's pigs. Illicit sex and other popular entanglements know nothing of the deadly seriousness of the elemental land, decorated with pigs' snouts rooting up fences and ploughing up lawns. Murderous thought and a shotgun go arm in arm, in the twilight, among the birches, along the elms, by the river.

Then in the early hours of one morning, when presumably concentration and meditation could go no farther even in nightmare, thought got choked down and the mind rose up and broke through -into the void: and the void lit up. The light was quiet and the only object visible was the brain of the enemy in the shape of moving plates each about the size of a small story book, but whitish in colour and smooth like damp ice. As the man watched the movement he became aware of every thought in that enemy head. A fine transparency was completely revealing of thought, character, personal idiosyncrasy. The understanding was so complete that the man was touched; and he became aware of himself there, too, a self-awareness that was absolute and pleasant while his vision continued to interpenetrate the smooth easy movements of the plates, of the head around them, and somehow of the man himself, now no longer the enemy. But what needs stressing was not simply the conviction but the absolute certainty that here was revelation, final truth. From now on there would be complete relaxation, easy movements in freedom, and an amused foresight of how to deal successfully with all future events and encounters. And this is exactly what happened. "I even got, at times, a certain affection for the crafty old devil." (But he could not tell at what point in this experience he had passed from sleep into full wakefulness).

A study of just how this insight affected the man's relations with his fellow men as time went on might be interesting, particularly when it came to deal with the virtues that are not exclusively Christian. For instance, to forgive your enemies, to do good to them that hate you and the like, become almost meaningless, futile injunctions – even unnecessarily dangerous (by increasing repression, inhibition) – without first understanding your enemy and yourself. It's not turning the other cheek that matters, it's so presenting and exposing the situation that turning the other cheek isn't necessary. Where understanding is complete hatred is impossible.

And again, as with the crocus, the effects of the insight will penetrate into other regions, lighting up what had been dark and fearful. I remember, many years ago, writing about some French authors like Jean-Paul Sartre, who had created that haunting being called the Other, and sometimes the Eye – the Eye that confronts one's loneliness, and sucks one's substance away. To me the idea that every Other has this kind of Eye seemed a monstrous generalisation of the ancient Evil Eye. In primitive communities there might be one who was considered to have this disintegrating Eye, male or female, demon or witch or bloodsucking vampire. But always it was one among many. The notion that every Other person has this kind of Eye, until as a final refinement the person disappears leaving only the Eye, would have been inconceivable to the ordinary members of any community. That's not the way things were, in simple fact. In much of the literature given over to this sort of mythologising of a primitive attitude or belief, this universalising of a particular instance in such unwarranted and unnatural fashion, it should not be surprising that the destructive elements are present in force from the perversions and masochisms of sex to the ultimate reaches of a depersonalising corrosive cynicism, and that any display of the positive virtues like goodness, kindness, natural love, would be felt as a disgusting intrusion. But the medical history of any advanced manic-depressive case makes this clear. What's of interest in my simple story of the man and his enemy is that it dealt with the particular instance, with an actual experience, and the dark destructive tangle was dissipated by the light of an insight. Simply and factually the insight got results, where no analysis or other reasoned explanation of any kind I can think of would have done.

But in all this one is up against the difficulty of communication. I have long taken for granted that if you experience an intuitive apprehension of some such kind and dimension as I have been talking about and try to convey it to another who has never experienced anything of the sort you'll fail and leave him with the impression that you are confused or worse – and, of course, you perfectly understand him and won't do it again. Sometimes, however, you quite fail to communicate the scope of a particular bout of intuition (illumination, enlightenment). For example, early in this rambling talk I used so many words to describe an experiment by American scientists that I felt I must not pile on more words in an effort to evoke the vision, the vision splendid, of an extra circle to consciousness, or an extra dimension to being, particularly as I had caught little more than an intimation, a flashing vision (felt as much as seen), within a universal vastness. You know the poet who saw eternity the other night.

Two final simple observations. The first is that in my experience there are far more people who have had some degree of enlightenment than is generally believed, and an odd one with intuitions of such intensity and penetration that one's own can feel very limited in comparison. The second would try to answer any practical question about whether intuitions have any lasting effect or finally serve any useful purpose.

Intuitions of varying degrees of vision and scope come and go, but I am convinced they leave something of themselves behind, and this something gets reinforced every time an intuition is recollected with the original clarity and freshness, and because of this it casts its blessing on the new incident or situation that evoked it. Thus its own small world of delight spreads.

Finally, then, an exercise in concentration, meditation and contemplation increases the chances of being struck by intuitions, intuitions on the way to a final enlightenment. But it's impossible in this region to do any neat packaging. For instance, I realise at this point – now – that after my first mention of the word contemplation I forgot it altogether. Possibly this last of the Yoga trio has never appealed to my ear, or its shape, its bowed head, to my eye. Too solemn – like George Fox's light (of which I know very little, so please meditate it for me!) Anyway, all that happened was that the purple of the crocus lit up 'the way' and kept me going. Don't try for too much at once in heaven's name. An intuition now and then prepares the ground. And by ground I don't mean the metaphysical Ground of being, but a vision of the simple earth where things grow, like grass and daisies, under the sun. A landscape that retains the light and is there waiting to receive you on your dark dead days. That's the abiding wonder of it. Entering into it your eyes look and lift, and within the wonder the wild geese have not flown away, the crocus has not died.

23

The Miraculous

WHEN I FIRST read *In Search of the Miraculous,* by P. D. Ouspensky, I was held as by a first-rate novel; continuously interesting, often exciting, always unexpected, and with the Bolshevik Revolution as background. Fundamentally it was – it is – a true tale of adventure, a hunt through the forests of the human mind, following new psychological trails, discarding most of our modern ones, new yet so old that at the start Ouspensky is heading for India in order to track down the ancient esoteric schools of the East. To his friends he said he was off to 'seek the miraculous'. Though unable to define 'miraculous' it yet had for him a definite meaning, for he had 'come to the conclusion a long time ago that there was no escape from the labyrinth of contradictions in which we live except by an entirely new road… I already knew then as an undoubted fact that beyond this thin film of false reality there existed another reality from which, for some reason, something separated us. The 'miraculous' was the way of penetration into this unknown reality'.

Though he had some notable Eastern experiences, he failed to penetrate to his unknown reality; the secret was more deeply hidden than he had supposed. But then he had made it difficult for himself, because schools of a religious kind did not attract him (plenty of them in Russia), other schools with 'very nice' people, of a slightly moral philosophical type (sentimental with a shade of asceticism), did not possess 'real knowledge'; even 'Yogi schools', complete with trance states, savoured of 'spiritualism' and he could not trust them; and he was

136

suspicious of what Orthodox mystics called 'beauty' or allurement. In short, whatever a school was called-occult, esoteric or Yogi – he wanted it to exist on the 'ordinary earthly plane', like any other kind of school. To think of schools on 'another plane' was a sign of weakness, of dreams instead of real search, and such 'dreams were one of the principal obstacles on our possible way to the miraculous'.

Plainly this journalist, author, original thinker, and fine mathematician, was on a difficult quest, yet when at last he returned to Russia on the outbreak of the first world war he still believed as profoundly as ever in the existence of his unknown reality.

Then one day, while at work on a Moscow newspaper, he came on an advertisement of the scenario of a ballet, 'The Struggle of the Magicians'' belonging to a certain 'Hindu'. The ballet was to take place in India, complete with 'Oriental magic, fakir miracles, sacred dances'. Everything, he commented, which travellers go to India to see but never do. After quitting journalism, he started lecturing on his Indian travels in Petersburg, and here he was told of a Moscow group engaged in 'occult' investigations and experiments, and directed by a certain G., a Caucasian Greek – who turned out to be none other than the 'Hindu' of the ballet advertisement. So Ouspensky was not impressed. Of 'self-suggested' wonders he knew enough, including the ladies who suddenly see 'eyes' in their rooms, which float and fascinate them from street to street until they arrive at the house of the Oriental to whom the eyes belong. Only after persistent efforts by one of his new acquaintances did he agree to meet G. (Gurdjieff). From the moment of the meeting Ouspensky's whole way of life was changed.

The meeting took place in a small cafée where dealers and commission agents met. Among this noisy crew, G., with the face of an Indian raja or Arab sheik, no longer young, with his black moustache, piercing eyes, black overcoat, velvet collar and black bowler, seemed to the astonished Ouspensky to be disguised. When, later, G. took him to the house where his pupils were awaiting him, he said that his work interested many well-known people in Moscow, but when Ouspensky asked for their names he remained silent, even though Ouspensky explained that as a native of Moscow he knew most of the famous. The flat and its few pupils also fell short of what he had been led to expect. So altogether he plainly had the feeling that there was something unusual or uncertain about the whole set-up. Yet there was no uncertainty at all about his desire to meet G. again.

So they met and talked and Ouspensky records, in English of a remarkable directness and clarity, G.'s answers to all his questions Thus step by step the long journey began to what Ouspensky increasingly believed might be the unknown reality.

But it was not a steady progression. Each subject as it cropped up in the school or group in Petersburg or Moscow roused discussions that ran so contrary to our Western notions of meaning and understanding that a lot of time was required simply to get used to their strangeness; even the thousand dollars which G. asked from each pupil by way of school fee rather shocked (as G. expected) those who dissociated cash from the things of the spirit.

But perhaps, at this point, an extract from the first real discussion Ouspensky had with G. may best indicate the unvarying unexpectedness of subject matter and the always lucid methods of explication. Also the extract may presently provide a specific text for a piece of personal research into it, because the book itself is so crammed with marvels of thought and experience that merely to mention them would occupy my whole space.

Ouspensky, then, on an occasion when he had just returned from London, initiates a discussion by remarking, 'People are turning into machines. And no doubt sometimes they become perfect machines. But I do not believe they can think. If they tried to think, they could not have been such fine machines'.

But G. said that was 'only partly true. It depends first of all on the question *which* mind they use for their work. If they use the proper mind they will be able to think even better in the midst of all their work with machines. But, again, only if they think with the proper mind'.

(Ouspensky tells us he did not understand what G. meant by 'proper mind' and understood it only 'much later'.)

'And secondly', G. continued, 'the mechanisation you speak of is not at all dangerous. A man may be a man while working with machines. There is another kind of mechanisation which is much more dangerous: being a machine oneself. Have you ever thought about the fact that all peoples *themselves* are machines?'

'Yes', I said, 'from the strictly scientific point of view all people are machines governed by external influences. But the question is, can the scientific point of view be wholly accepted?'

'Scientific or not scientific is all the same to me" said G. 'I want you to understand what I am saying. Look, all these people you see', he pointed along the street, 'are simply machines – nothing more'.

'I think I understand what you mean', I said. 'And I have often thought how little there is in the world that can stand against this form of mechanisation and choose its own path'.

'This is just where you make your greatest mistake', said G. 'You think there is something that chooses its own path, something that can stand against mechanisation; you think that not everything is equally mechanical'.

'Why, of course not!' I said. 'Art, poetry, thought, are phenomena of quite a different order'.

'Of exactly the same order'' said G. 'These activities are just as mechanical as everything else. Men are machines and nothing but mechanical actions can be expected of machines'.

But Ouspensky replies that people are so unlike one another that they cannot all be brought under the same heading: 'there are savages, there are mechanical people, there are intellectual people, there are geniuses'.

'Quite right', replied G., 'people are very unlike one another, but the real difference of which you speak simply does not exist. This must be understood. All the people you see, all the people you know, all the people *you may get to know*, are machines, actual machines, working solely under the power of external influences, as you yourself said. Machines they are born and machines they die. How do savages and intellectuals come into this? Even now, at this very moment, while we are talking, several millions of machines are trying to annihilate one another. What is the difference between them? Where are the savages, and where are the intellectuals? They are all alike.… But there is a possibility of ceasing to be a machine. It is of this we must think'.

And in a subsequent conversation when Ouspensky wants to talk of psychology, G. interrupts him: 'Before speaking of psychology we must be clear to whom it refers and to whom it does not refer. *Psychology* refers to people, to men, to human beings. What *psychology* can there be in relation to machines? Mechanics, not psychology, is necessary for the study of 'machines. That is why we begin with mechanics. It is a very long way yet to psychology'.

'Can one stop being a machine?'

'Ah! That is the question. If you had asked such questions more often we might perhaps have got somewhere'.

So the remorseless process goes on, onslaught after onslaught upon old attitudes and beliefs. Often Ouspensky fails to understand, cannot accept, but G.'s assurance is never for a moment at a loss. It proceeds from point to point with a simplicity, a logic, that seems to emanate from a higher level of being, uncoloured by individual subjective feelings, always objective. And if this never fails to astonish in the realm of man s behaviour and beliefs on earth, when it takes off from the earthly for the cosmological it becomes so fantastic that one's fundamental nature rebels against what appears so manifestly incredible. Yet G.'s presentation remains as lucid and complete as ever. Even Ouspensky, who is an expert in the cosmological realm and has written profoundly about it, can but sit and try to take it all in. For more and more as question or subject is discussed, he realises that what G. is giving them are fragments of a whole universally integrated system, towards which he may in time lead them, as they apprehend in some measure this fragment or that, and so lessen the grip of the mechanical upon them. And this in itself is more than strange for as the sessions of talk go on, the more it is made clear that one of G.'s fundamental ideas concerns 'the complete materiality of all the psychic, intellectual, emotional, and other inner processes, including the most exalted poetic inspirations, religious ecstasies, and mystical revelations'. There is no let off or let down, no easing into warm sentiment. Even the meaning of the word 'materiality' is buttressed with statistical tables and diagrams.

But to get the full impact of G.'s concept of mechanical man we must get some idea of the two lines along which man's development proceeds, the line of *knowledge* and the line of *being*. We can all understand that there are different levels of knowledge but we accept *being* as merely another name for existence. In our culture we put great value upon levels of man's knowledge, but normally ignore the level of his being, as in the case of an able scientist who while notably advancing science may be – and has the right to be – a 'petty, egoistic, caviling, mean, envious, vain, naive, and absent-minded man'. Seemingly a professor 'must always forget his umbrella everywhere'. For we do not understand that being has its different levels just like knowledge. It is only when the two interact in harmony that we have enrichment of *being* and an increase in its capacity to absorb ever more *knowledge* and to transmute it into *understanding*. When this does not happen man continues to live in *sleep*. When knowledge develops without being you have a 'weak Yogi', when being develops without knowledge, a 'stupid saint'.

But as I have already said it is impossible to give in small space the range of fascinating material that never fails to astonish and disturb, so I thought it might be an interesting experiment at this point if I took by way of text two words which are italicised and crop up fairly often. Clearly they are key words designed to unlock the mechanical in man and to awake him from his sleep. The two words are 'remember yourself'. At first they meant little to me yet were vaguely disturbing. On the surface, as G. said, to tell a man that he could not remember himself was absurd. Of course a man, every man, can remember himself. Idiotic to say anything else! But Ouspensky, though unable to get any real meaning, decided during an exercise in self-observation (basic in G.'s system) to try to *remember himself*, and did come to the conclusion that in fact we never do remember ourselves. This was amazing enough, but, more amazing, he soon was profoundly convinced that he 'was faced with *an entirely new problem which science and philosophy had not, so far, come across*'. (His italics). He drew diagrams to help fix this elusive remembering. Then he experimented by saying '*I* am walking. *I* am doing'. And realised that when he tried to hang on to the *I*, thought stopped. Yet it had nothing in common with 'self-feeling' or 'self-analysis'. It was new and had a new flavour. Of course this kind of experimenting and talk about it rouses little interest in another unless he feels some degree of response. If there is no response it all becomes just boring. But here I was not at all bored because I had already found that when I had tried to communicate to someone an experience which he had never had, I failed. Applying this now to myself I realised that it was the word 'remember' that blocked the line of communication to me. As I read on, however, I found that Ouspensky had been familiar with 'moments of self-remembering' since childhood and while travelling in a new place had experienced a momentary sensation of strangeness in finding himself there. This sensation I perfectly understood. Often while on foot in the Highlands, in turning a corner, in opening out a vista, I had been stopped in breathless wonder at the scene before me. But this wonder was pervaded by the wonder of finding myself there. This *I* – this *me* – here! Certainly it had nothing to do with memory. On the contrary it was as if you had found yourself for the first time. Here is not the ordinary self of everyday, but a new self, at once incredibly intimate and utterly undemanding, fresh as the first view of creation. Here at last is the *conscious* self.

Something like this, it would appear, had happened to Ouspensky, though less than ever could I understand why he called it 'remembering yourself'. But what was very clear was that Ouspensky perceived more and more its tremendous significance, and called it the centre of gravity of G.'s whole system while declaring that western psychology had entirely overlooked it. We 'live and act in deep sleep, not metaphorically but in absolute reality'. But 'we *can* remember ourselves if we make sufficient efforts, we *can* awaken'.

Yet still the ambiguity of his 'remembering' remained. In fact he seemed to stress the memory part, the effect the experience had on the memory. And of course it makes an indelible impression on the memory once one has had it. However, with me this particular kind of experience was an old one. Indeed I wrote about it years ago and spontaneously called this self you come upon the Second Self, the first being the ordinary everyday self. And this second self could regard the doings and antics of the first self with a detachment that held complete understanding.

But theorising and imagining are never enough. There must be ever more actual experience that produces this effect of becoming aware of oneself, of becoming *conscious* in this new and illuminating way. And this experience may not be involuntary, a sheer gift from Nature and the Arts; it may come at a profound level only after a fight through darkness with a terrific exercise of the will. One must *do*, as G. never forgets to stress. So let me try to illustrate this aspect of becoming *conscious*, of breaking through the mechanical to the conscious self, by telling two stories, two actual happenings.

The first concerns a man and his wife who had fallen out. It was a case of the poet's simple disappointment becoming in a few moments a theme for Sophocles, for they had a deep mutual affection. But now the disagreement began to enlarge itself, with ever more and more implications seeping in, until it gave a few 'reasonable' if, on his part, impatient words, a significance that began to clot the very core of life in a dumb and dark way. Finally, before something terrible, unforgivable, could be said he got up, went out, found his spade and tackled the earth. It was all absurd; it was maddening; still, damn it, there was a limit! … The more he tried for an iron control the darker all grew; the darkness began to embody itself … he had a dark sight of devil swirls…. of wrestling with the Devil… religious imagery! My God, what next?… Because this was getting beyond absurdity it became a struggle within himself, his wife forgotten. But he found he didn't want to win…he wanted to enjoy the luxury of letting the devil win… So he struggled against the devil with all his might, for he *must* win, to show he could not be beaten, to prove the strength of his will. He would strangle the devil first before getting back to his wife. He hung on… and suddenly the darkness broke, the tension eased, the light came through-and all was calm, simple, delightful. The incredible relief of it! The light itself smiling. He could see in one glance every thing that had happened with a wonderful clarity, saw his wife's essential and everlasting nature, loved the very thought of it…. then saw his own nature, its essenceÉand became *conscious*, as it seemed for the first time, of this permanent self within him, and, in the same moment of realisation, became conscious of his wife's permanent self in the same way. Sheer revelation of what forever endured, however obscured by mechanical happenings, chance moods, in the world of everyday. 'There was a sort of radiant quiet humour in it, too', he added.

Now this did seem to reinforce G.'s general attitude regarding man's mechanical nature and the tremendous difficulty of recognising it and deliberately dealing with it. It also confirmed G.'s contention that ordinary mechanical man was not one unchanging 'I'. The 'I' that exists now will become an entirely different 'I' later on. The friendly 'I' of the afternoon blushes with embarrassment at the angry 'I' of the forenoon. By the following day it may be a piece of walking misery, and, the day after, it sinks its putt for a win on the last green and becomes triumphant. Hundreds of different 'I's in the course of a week. Chance happenings; mechanical responses; no permanent 'I'.

But perhaps a personal experience may take Ouspensky's 'entirely new problem which science and philosophy had not so far come across' a step further. It is very difficult to describe simply, as exceptional conditions of mind have to be evoked. It was also very involved because it was not a direct happening, not a first-hand encounter, but arose while I was engaged in writing a culminating part of a novel. The character involved in the novel had fallen down a cliff in trying to save a lamb, but the lamb saved him by getting squashed under his body in the final impact. He had crawled to a cave, failed to meet 'the wild man', a solitary of that remote mountainous district of the Highlands, underwent crucial mental experiences, and at last set out on a final hopeless crawl. Perhaps it was because I knew the country that I began to identify myself abnormally with my character.

I saw what he saw, became as it were the seeing person; improvised his crutch, suffered what he suffered, until in one translated moment, in a look back at the mountain slopes, the swinging footbridge over the gorge, I saw a face, larger than life size, looking down at me with an expression of infinite understanding and compassion, still, not doing anything, not going to do anything, there. The effect upon me was of an intimacy I could never express, for the face was my own face.

Though I have read many psychiatrists' reports on the effects of LSD and other drugs, I have never actually taken any myself. My experience was for me therefore all the more arresting, as it occurred in daylight, on the clear air and not even against a physical background of mountains and birch trees which might have contributed to the creation of an illusory effect. Indeed I forgot, even in the moment of writing this, that the illusion or 'projection' took place in my writing room while my mind was concentrated on its creative task. However, there is no need to complicate the affair but merely to make my point that I had what was for me a clear vision of my second self looking down the few yards of sloping ground at my first self prostrate in the heather and now held by an understanding and compassion that were infinite. Then the infinite itself came elusively in and the second self became a part, a manifestation, of a universal self or essence, a part of, yet individual.

Did G.'s injunction to 'remember yourself' take in such experiences as I have tried to describe? Long after, I came to the conclusion that it did; indeed a book was subsequently published by Ouspensky in which he said that memory did not really come into the injunction, though that was after he had parted from G. Today as I look over the 'miraculous' book after many years I find it as fascinating as ever, and charged with profundities I had all but forgotten, any one of which could well provide a new text for individual research into the unknown reality.

The wonder of it all is that once one does begin to penetrate into meaning and significance there seems to be no end to it. For the concern here is not with academic considerations of history, philosophy, metaphysics, religion (though there is just an indication that G. may have inhabited far regions of *esoteric* Christianity), but with man's development from his present level of knowledge and being onto higher levels; not analyses for learning's sake, not theorising, but *doing*. Doing is one of his loaded words. 'Doing is magic', said G.

The further one goes in development the more magical the prospect becomes. The breakthrough from mechanical man even into a momentary apprehension of his permanent self lights up a new world, where his own judgment comes more and more confidently into play. Often now he will be astonished that he had altogether missed the true meaning of a saying or piece of writing which he thought he had thoroughly understood. Even individual words like insight or intuition take on new and profounder implications.

But again to illustrate such assertions let me take a quotation I came across a few days ago. One more experience from an individual. By many Braque is considered the greatest artist of our age. Here is what he said 'Reality only reveals itself when it is illuminated by a ray of poetry. All around us is asleep'. I need not remark on my reaction of near shock to the word 'asleep'! The word that would once upon a time have seemed vague, overdone, and factually untrue was now charged with precise meaning, not to mention a certain pervasive humour. But though that brief quotation could be a text for whole pages in the G. manner, I should like to draw attention only to its opening words, 'Reality reveals itself'. It is not that Reality 'is revealed', but that it 'reveals itself'. If it were 'revealed' it would be seen so to speak in outline, objectively, but when it 'reveals itself'' it has a radiance, a radiance that seems to come towards one out of a realm of boundless freedom and delight. Now once again I find myself amid insights, intuitions, enlightenment, as *I* endeavoured to evoke them under the title *Light* in the last issue of this magazine. The same reality (or Reality), with the same utter certainty that this is the final reality. And if 'certainty' here is a difficult word, it has to be experienced to be understood.

Finally, it was at this point in my hunt of 'remember yourself' that there involuntarily arose in me a first suggestion of criticism of G.'s system. I had gone far enough apparently for something like this to happen. I began to sense, to feel, that something was lacking, a lack of warmth, an indulgence in mathematical and diagrammatic explanation at the expense of radiance, delight, freedom. That overstates, yet for me it began to hold some sort of fundamental significance. Vistas would open up – and vanish. What I had experienced so far was very little, nothing, compared with the vast unknown ahead. Within that vastness G.'s system should complete itself, become a unified whole, a Unity, like Braque's Reality. But that implied the attainment of levels of being in the G. system which the utmost stretch of my mind could not begin to entertain. And at the same time, and throughout all this, a certain small wormish doubt kept me wondering why Ouspensky, after years of work on the system, at last found it impossible to continue his association with G. It could not be the work itself for clearly Ouspensky liked nothing better than using mathematics and inventing diagrams to complete G.'s system. It must have been something at a much deeper level, and this is what I strove to understand. But here Ouspensky's natural reticence did not help though it was disturbing; it gave no real clue; though G.'s actions at this point in the matter of discontinuing the school showed a personal unrest of an arbitrary and peculiar kind. My mind goes back to when we first meet him as the advertised master of a ballet of magicians. When they fled from the Bolsheviks, G. set up a new ballet school that achieved some considerable fame at Fontainebleau near Paris. Ouspensky went to London and continued the work there on his own. So in the end I had to ask myself, among many questions, this question: Was G.'s system never finally realisable, not even by G.? The scope of the question precludes any possible answer from me. All I can be sure of is that when Ouspensky had written his book, *In Search of the Miraculous*, he gave it for a subtitle *Fragments of an Unknown Teaching*. Fragments, not Unity.

Afterword

Landscape to Light, the title chosen for this collection of essays by Neil M. Gunn, one of Scotland's greatest twentieth-century novelists, can be understood as a miniature biography of the author himself.[1] Gunn drew inspiration from the landscape of the Highlands of Scotland, a land he knew deeply and intimately, and used it to nourish his thinking in a creative life that spanned the Depression, the Second World War and the early years of the Cold War. The essays, inextricably linked to the novels, reflect a development of Gunn's mental landscape from a keen sense of observation of the land and people he loved to a hunt for the improvement of the human lot in a troubled world and, perhaps more importantly, for enlightenment on a personal level and the realisation of self. Although best known as a profound and successful novelist, Gunn was a perceptive essayist, and many of the ideas explored in his essays find their way into the novels. An essay by its very nature, brief enough to be read in a single sitting, and structured to focus on the elaboration of a single theme, is restricted and cannot cover as much ground as a novel; a collection of essays, however, can equal in scope and depth a serious novel. The essays in *Landscape to Light* do just that, mapping Gunn's own journey from the Highland landscape to that other country of the mind and spirit.

The Caithness community into which Gunn was born in 1891 was warm and friendly and traditionally Highland. Gunn was to write:

> Caithness is a triangle whose base had to be glued on to the county of Sutherland by a range of mountains, but whose other two sides are open to the

sea; at least they characteristically confront the sea with sheer contorted battling cliffs. (*Country Fair*, December 1956)

His father, a fishing boat skipper, enjoyed the reputation of being both adventurous and successful. Fishing, however, was in decline and none of the seven boys in the family followed his father to sea. Three emigrated to Canada and four (including Neil Gunn) took up careers in the Civil Service and teaching. As a boy of obvious brilliance and ability, Gunn was to leave the local primary school in his native village of Dunbeath to pursue his education at the hands of a private tutor employed by an elder sister and her doctor husband in Kirkcudbrightshire in the south west of Scotland. From there Gunn entered the Civil Service and worked both in London and Edinburgh before qualifying as an excise officer. After a brief spell in England he was assigned to a post in Lybster, a fishing village in his native Caithness. His career in Customs and Excise was interrupted by the First World War, but the work in which he was involved for the Admiralty kept him in the Highlands, where he was to remain for the rest of his life. While working for the Customs and Excise Gunn struck up a friendship with the Irishman, Maurice Walsh. They both took up writing and when Walsh returned to Ireland their friendly rivalry and encouragement continued with Walsh's first book *The Key Above the Door* being published the same year as *The Grey Coast* (1926). Walsh was to become a prolific and popular novelist and drew on Gunn's support in elaborating details of plot.

Although his early literary life in terms of writing poems, essays and short stories began during his period of First World War work, the essential stimulus for Gunn's more mature writing was his reaction to the Caithness he found on his return there in 1922. He saw the county he had so lovingly known as a child in steep economic decline. Neglected farms and crofts, silted-up harbours, fewer fishing boats and poor roads filled him with a profound sense of shock and bitterness. It took two novels, *The Grey Coast* and *The Lost Glen* (1932), to exorcise this feeling of something lost. The novels reflect the dire economic situation of the crofting and fishing communities and the demeaning aspect of some of the work undertaken by the local people to cater for the needs of the fishing and shooting fraternity of landowners and wealthy visitors. The bleakness of the subject matter in these works helped temper, if not eradicate, the 'Celtic Twilight' influence in Gunn's early writing. Gunn had also joined the National Party of

Scotland on its foundation in 1929 and over the coming years was instrumental in bringing about the merging of the National Party of Scotland with the Scottish Party to form the Scottish National Party. His passionate awareness of the injustices of the past and present shaped the mood of the early novels but Gunn, by nature a positive man, looked for cooperation, freedom and hope. This positive outlook dominates his third book, *Morning Tide* (1931), written after *The Lost Glen* but published before it, reflecting the author's determination that there was something in the psyche of the local people that could restore their belief in themselves and to move forward in different ways.[2] It was a book deeply influenced by recollections of his own boyhood and one that anticipated two books that were to become modern classics, *Highland River* (1937) and *The Silver Darlings* (1941). All these books are set in Caithness but Gunn never saw himself as a regional novelist.

> Though I spent most of my teenage years in London and Edinburgh there was never any doubt in my mind when I started writing that the highlands and Islands comprised the basis of what mattered in depth and wonder for me. Not, of course, in any exclusive sense but simply that from this culture all other cultures could be looked at.[3]

It is appropriate that the first essay in *Landscape to Light* is entitled 'Caithness and Sutherland'. Written in 1935 after the initial success of the novel *Morning Tide*, it contains the germs of ideas that were to be developed in many of his novels. Early in the essay, which could be described as a guidebook for the cultivated and discerning tourist, he describes an approach to Thurso from the mountainous and dramatic scenery of the West.

> From that background, or as it were from that door, you walk out upon Caithness, and at once experience an austerity in the flat clean windswept lands that affects the mind almost with a sense of shock. There is something more in it than contrast. It is a movement of the spirit that finds in the austerity, because strength is there also, a final serenity. I know of no other landscape in Scotland that achieves this harmony, that in the very moment of purging the mind of its dramatic grandeur, leaves it free and ennobled. The Pentland Firth, outreaching on the left, is of a blueness that I, at least, failed to find in the Mediterranean; a living blueness, cold-glittering in the sun and smashed to gleaming snowdrift on the bows of the great rock battle-ships of the Orkneys, bare and austere also. The wind of time has searched out even the flaws and cleansed them. (p. 2–3)

In this evocative and powerful piece of writing about a northern landscape, the land and sea seem to have a personality of their own, both strong and serene, and the author an extraordinary sense of awareness of the effect of environment on the perceptive and sympathetic viewer. 'East to Buchan' journeys along the Moray coast visiting the fishing villages and witnessing the slow decline of a once booming industry. It confirms this ability to capture and convey both landscape and those who work within it.

In 'My Bit of Britain' he again shows a deep sense of rootedness to this austere land and menacing sea, but introduces a sombre thought in the form of exposing the powerlessness of those living in this part of Scotland in the face of economic forces over which they have no control. The Clearances, the forced depopulation of the glens to make way for sheep farming in the eighteenth and early nineteenth centuries, are a well known example of this and represent a bleak period of Highland history, impregnated with cruelty and a sense of betrayal and depicted by Gunn in his 1934 novel *Butcher's Broom*. 'One Fisher Went Sailing' was written at the same time as *Off in a Boat* (1938), both drawing on his journey down the west coast of Scotland. The essay looks closely at the economic, social and environmental pressures on the fishing industry. Neil Gunn was making observations and gathering research that would feed the detail and vision of his epic of the herring industry *The Silver Darlings* (1941). Essay and novel embody the sense, found also in the writings of Patrick Geddes, of the integration of place, work and community, a theme that recurs throughout Gunn's work.

By the later 1930s Gunn had moved away from the concerns of nationalism and the bitterness of periods such as the Clearances to the plight of the descendants of those dispossessed people and to the communities struggling with the decline of the fishing industry. Less emotive than the Clearances and not so widely known is the effect Government legislation in various forms had on the lives of fishermen during the same period, and even later in the twentieth century. In that century Britain's foreign policy with regard to the newly fledged Soviet Russia spelt the end of the lucrative trade that Scottish fishermen had enjoyed with the Baltic area. Westminster policy, on the other hand, could be benevolent as was shown during the Napoleonic wars when every encouragement was given to developing the herring industry, a subject well covered in 'The Wonder Story of the Moray Firth'.[4] What can be easily gleaned from these essays is that although the sea is free, the conditions for those who fish its waters are prey to benevolent or malevolent decisions made elsewhere. This underlines the importance of traditional community life to preserve within itself all that is meaningful and life enhancing.

Gunn's fascination by the sea and its potential freedom is beautifully captured in 'The French Smack'. That he should have admired a foreign competitor trespassing in Scottish waters says much for his admiration for those who make their living on the capricious sea. More than that, he sees in the daring of the French smack a flouting of authority and a sense of freedom that the sea inspires. In this he evokes the spirit of Joseph Conrad in that author's admiration of those who depend for their living on the sea. This idea of fundamental freedom is preserved in an essay that leaves the immensity of the sea for the intimacy of the land, and a stream that flows through it. In 'The First Salmon' he puts over so refreshingly the primordial instinct of man on the hunt in the form of a fishing expedition at the beginning of the season. His excitement of this simple pursuit comes through strongly and hauntingly in his description of the first pool to be fished.

> Down through some beeches and over grey grass and yellow moss, there was the first pool, dark moving water with white flicks and ripples. How lovely a thing a fishing pool is. It has intimacy and ancestry in it. (p. 42)

This chimes with Kenn's battle with the salmon in the opening of *Highland River* (1937). Gunn writes this in a world that is poised for conflict and cannot but muse on war and peace. He describes peace not as an absence of war but as a living reality.

> A positive thing like the scent of the beeches and the ling, or the first notes of a young chaffinch, or the cry of a newly arrived peewit – or the song of a reel. (p. 42)

The success of *Highland River*, winner of the James Tait Black Memorial Prize, enabled Gunn to take up the challenge of becoming a full-time writer. He resigned from his Civil Service post, bought a boat, and set off on the journey down the west coast of Scotland noted above. The experiences and observations on this voyage resulted in the book *Off in a Boat* (1938). From the freedom of the fishing smack and the fishing rod Gunn moves again to a subject that is always lingering in the conscious or subconscious memory of the Highlander – the Clearances. 'Black Cattle in Lochaber' is a bitter-sweet essay that shows what could be done by a landlord pursuing the true Celtic tradition of chieftainship. There is a sadness about it as it is only a prelude to a dark period of ejection of peoples from ancestral lands; it shows the ultimate impotence of a caring chief attempting to combat forces of both an economic and social nature. What is of the greatest import in the essay is the death of a civilisation betrayed from within. Disposses-sion, suffering and exile are so easily invoked by the landscape of the North through its endless moors and deserted glens.

On settling in a farmhouse on the hills near Dingwall, the county town of Ross and Cromarty, he wrote two novels comparatively quickly, *Wild Geese Overhead* (1939) and *Second Sight* (1940), one set in contemporary Glasgow and the other in a shooting lodge in the Highlands. In both novels considerable scope is given to dialogue or general discussion on matters of political, social and philosophical interest in such diverse places as the pubs of Glasgow and the dinner table of a shooting lodge. The contents of the six essays, 'On Backgrounds', 'On Tradition', 'On Belief', 'On Looking at Things', 'On Magic', and 'On Destruction', all written in 1940 and 1941, reflecting his views and those of thinking people in a period of crisis and uncertainty, indirectly inform his contemporaneous novels and influence many of his later works. The essays, despite their brevity and focus, offer the advantage of revealing many of Gunn's thoughts directly. In 'On Backgrounds' he extols the virtues of living and creative backgrounds and sees any feeling of superiority in a tradition leading to cultural isolation and an atrophy of being in its exponents; in 'On Tradition' he sees the importance of uncovering traditions that may have been driven underground in order to bring back vitality and meaningful living to communities; in 'On Belief' he expresses detestation for modern ideologies, systems and movements – all derivatives of arid intellectualism – and extols the virtues of good personal relations and reverence for life; in 'On Looking at Things' he encourages the reader to detach himself or herself from the hurly-burly of modern life to look in a new way at the wonders of creation; in 'On Magic' Gunn takes the side of the intuitive and inexplicable feelings of the heart against any rigid belief in the ultimate supremacy of logic and rationality and in 'On Destruction' he ponders the simple games of cowboys and Indians played by boys of his generation, in which the emphasis was on field craft rather than on the simulation of killing and destruction in the games of the War years.

The 1940s would see Gunn in the prime of his writing career. He was now settled in Braefarm House near Dingwall and, despite the wartime shortages of materials, books and reading matter were in great demand. During this period he wrote ten novels including *The Silver Darlings* (1941), *The Serpent* (1943), and *The Green Isle of the Great Deep* (1944). He also wrote numerous essays, political, topical, and rural. The series of rural essays on the life around Braefarm published in the *Scots Magazine* and *Chambers Journal* were collected in *Highland Pack* (1949).

A concrete revelation of Gunn's thinking comes in the essay 'The New Community of Iona', written, using the pseudonym of Dane McNeil, on the eve of the Second World War, in which Gunn applauds the efforts of a prominent Church of Scotland minister to establish a community on the holy island of Iona to revive the Columban idea of fellowship and communal life; he sees it as a creative move to meet the need within the church for a re-vitalising impulse. In addition, he sees this as a positive move against the increasing mechanisation of life, the loss of individual freedom under political tyrannies and the relentless movement towards the material in modern life that was robbing man of his dignity and life of its ecstasy. His final sentence, 'And Iona was the island of light', is an early pointer to the direction he would be taking in his literary and spiritual pilgrimage, a direction that would lead to concentration on the individual, the 'self'.

As J. B. Pick has noted, the poetry in Gunn's writing 'is not a matter of words but of perception' and throughout Gunn's writing career there had always been a tension between outer and inner action.[5] His readers had always desired and expected a strong perceptive and descriptive depiction of the world of the Highlands. But while Gunn was always aware of the requirements of his craft as a popular novelist, he was also drawn as a man and an artist to the inner meanings and landscapes of his subject. In his later works these inner landscapes come more to the fore and it is clear that Gunn's desire to keep writing was motivated by his forays into this territory.

Twenty years separate the writing of the essay on the social experiment in Iona from that of 'The Heron's Legs', a period during which Gunn wrote fifteen novels and a so-called spiritual autobiography, *The Atom of Delight*. The novels impress by their variety, their sense of search, be that in the nineteenth-century epic of the exciting period of the herring boom, *The Silver Darlings*, or in the timeless struggle between native wisdom and the suffocating conformity imposed by a totalitarian state in *The Green Isle of the Great Deep*. The setting for all his late books, apart from *The Lost Chart* (1949), remains the Highlands of Scotland. *The Well at the World's End* (1951) captures the spirit of his attitude to life and is a signpost to the final stages of Gunn's journey to self-realisation or Light.

> Where most novels of the ambitious kind today deal with violence and materialism leading to negation and despair, I thought it might be a change if I got a character who would wander among his fellows looking for the positive aspects of life. Is it possible to pierce the negative husk, the dark cloud, even for a few moments, and come on the light, the bubbling well at the end of the fairy tale?[26]

A few years after writing *The Well at the World's End* Gunn became seriously interested in Far Eastern philosophy, particularly Zen Buddhism, an interest that led to a correspondence with a Japanese academic who had been fascinated by certain aspects of Gunn's Highland experiences. An exchange of views with his Japanese contact and further reading on Zen thrilled Gunn; he perceived parallels between his own work and experiences and those of an alien tradition. All this was to affect the content and structure of his spiritual autobiography, *The Atom of Delight* (1956). The book focuses on separate episodes that act as launch pads for further thought. The inclusion of a piece on Zen comes as no surprise, particularly as it concerns a book, *Zen in the Art of Archery*, that was the key to Gunn's early insights into Zen. J. B. Pick had sent him a copy of Herrigel's book on its publication in 1953. Opening this book was as vital a moment in his pilgrimage as the episode describing a big salmon being landed by a little boy, an incident already described in one of Gunn's early masterpieces, *Highland River*. But it is in the chapter headed 'The Nut and the Stone' that shows most clearly that Gunn is on the way to self-realisation; it is a vivid and simple explanation of what Gunn understands as the true self or the second self.

> The shallow river flowed around and past with its variety of lulling monotonous sound; a soft wind, warmed by the sun, came upstream and murmured in my ears as it continuously slipped from my face. As I say, how I got there I do not remember. I do not even remember whether anyone had been with me on that expedition, much less what anxieties might have to be resolved with 'excuses' when I got home. I was just there.

> Then the next thing happened, and happened, so far as I can remember, for the first time. I have tried hard but can find no simpler way of expressing what happened than by saying: *I came upon myself sitting there.* (*The Atom of Delight*, p.29)

In 1956 Gunn was 65 and his habit of never writing the same book twice had always clashed with his publisher's desire for popular and tried formulas and Gunn now found himself very much out-of-step with the times. John Osborne and the novelist equivalent of 'angry young men' had captured the literary stage and Gunn's pursuit of the light was seen at best as escapism and at worst irrelevant to the age of the 'kitchen sink'. However, Gunn's quest for enlightenment and indeed his fascination with Zen Buddhism did not end with *The Atom of Delight*. Although it was goodbye to full-length books, he continued his search for light and delight in his later essays. He did not portray himself as an expert on Zen or attempt to describe what living by Zen meant, with its difficult conceptions of mortality, immortality and eternity. He wrote as someone who felt at ease and at home in the psychological territory explored by Zen. What he had come across in Zen merely confirmed consciously and subconsciously much of what he had been pursuing in his own particular pilgrimage.

In April 1958 Gunn heard from Alexander Reid the poet and dramatist who had just become editor of the *Saltire Review*. Reid had been impressed by the themes of *The Atom of Delight* and requested a series of essays in similar vein for the journal. There could be no better introduction to these essays almost exclusively focused on philosophical ideas than the one entitled 'The Heron's Legs'; it has a peculiar charm and delicacy of its own as Gunn reflects on a coloured print by a sixteenth-century Japanese artist, which shows a heron standing among reeds in a grey light. The essence of the bird and scene is captured by a few strokes of the artist's brush. It acted powerfully on Gunn in that it brought back intimate experiences he had had watching this bird in its Highland habitat. Such experiences had evoked an inexpressible feeling of wonder and a heightened awareness that enabled him to look at himself as part of the scene from without.

In 'The Flash' and 'Eight Times Up', both written in 1958, Gunn dwells further on his reaction to 'The Heron's Legs' before wandering into the psychological landscape of Zen.[7] He muses on the failure of Western methods of thinking and extols a way of thinking that was not linear, one dimensional and logical. Strangely enough, it is in the realm of advanced physics that he finds something analogous to the thoughts of Eastern thinkers dealing with the ultimate reaches of the mind. Certain absolutes are no longer accepted by the physicists, and with their dethronement, an element of uncertainty is introduced to this aspect of Western thinking. A blow to the inviolability of pure logic! Following this, Gunn introduces the ultimate experience of Zen: Satori. This is described as making the unconscious articulate. The articulated unconscious expresses itself in terms of logic incoherently – but most eloquently from the Zen point of view. This incoherency means an escape from the iron grip of intellectualism, and Gunn sees that escape through the finding of the essential 'I', the second self, a finding that is achieved for him through moments of sudden intense awareness or enlightenment.

'Landscape Inside' gives a clear idea of what landscape can mean to Gunn.

> I can't remember (though I may be wrong) ever having described a High-
> land scene for the scene's sake. Always the scene has something to do with
> the mind of the character who finds himself there. (p. 106)

Gunn develops this theme further, dwelling on his own experiences.

> … unless you come upon yourself in some such way, as an element present
> in the scene or landscape, the chances are that you will forget it, however
> long you look at it. (p. 110)

This may appear difficult to understand at first reading but it becomes clearer in the later essays in this collection in which Gunn looks to Far Eastern philosophy to interpret and confirm some of his own beliefs and experiences. 'Highland Space', itself a later essay, moves to the varied reaction of people of all backgrounds to the space offered to them in the Highlands in the form of mountains and endless moors.[8] Often the reaction is one of fear, a sort of horror of being exposed to an earthly manifestation of the 'infinite.' Gunn argues that although such a reaction is understandable in those used to the urban culture of the West, it need not be so in other cultures, and turns to Eastern philosophy where words like Emptiness, Nothingness, the Void are used quite commonly in a paradoxical sense. Although Gunn was writing this essay when he was at an advanced state of his spiritual pilgrimage, he never forsakes the idea of landscape as an essential ingredient in his search for self-realisation.

It would have been understandable if Gunn had decided to cease his exploration within Zen at this stage. It was not to be. A further stimulus to his never ending search came in the form of a book *In Search of the Miraculous* by a Russian writer, P. D. Ouspensky, a disciple of a well known and revered guru, Georges Gurdjieff. In 'Remember Yourself' Gunn explores this book and Gurdjieff's approach to inner development. The writer saw man as a piece of mechanism to which things happen and who works under the power of external influences; he is the unconscious man. The conscious man is the one who has come upon his own self, the 'I'. To make the unconscious man conscious he advocated a system in which the device of self-remembering was prominent. Gunn agrees with Gurdjieff's aim but stresses that his experiences of self-realisation have been entirely involuntary. Many of his traditional readers struggled to keep up with Gunn as he ventured into the inner landscapes of these later works and after the bafflement shown by some to his *Saltire Review* articles and the death of his companion and wife Daisy in 1963, Gunn confessed to feeling that he had 'written enough'.[9]

However, the pilgrimage was not over. J. B. Pick had maintained his written correspondence with Neil Gunn on a wide range of issues but particularly the notion of 'light' and 'insight'. This correspondence developed from the written word into the oral with the exchange of audiotapes. When Pick co-founded the journal *Point* in the late 1960s, he used one of these recordings as the basis of the essay 'Light' and as a spur to a further piece 'In Search of the Miraculous'. These final two essays continue the theme of 'Remember Yourself'. . In 'Light' he dwells on light and its varying degrees of intensity. His light is one of wonder, gaiety and laughter, in which all ordinary things are born afresh; he suggests a distinction between the quiet still light of ethical experience and the vivid flashing light of 'livingness'. His light has no place for words such as meaning and purpose; the insight or the light itself will be the meaning and the purpose. He is uneasy about Gurdjieff's assertion that the isolation of the 'I' can be achieved by spiritual techniques and thought processes and adheres to his belief in spontaneity of reflex and being taken by surprise by magical moments of light or insight, which explain his attraction to Zen. His observations on Zen are illuminating as he moves through the sunlit world of meditation, using koans (students' questions on meditation), Haiku verses, brief in structure and deep in significance, and the wonderful effects of light depicted by the Impressionists. All this prepares the reader for 'The Miraculous', which is a commentary on Ouspensky's *In Search of the Miraculous.* It reads like an adventure story of the mind. The interaction in thought between Gurdjieff and Ouspensky is absorbing. Their unflattering opinion of modern man (the unconscious man) reiterates that contained in *Remember Yourself.* There is a hint of a system of thought processes to make man more conscious, but this idea is not developed. Gunn's interest is aroused by Gurdjieff's penetrating insights, which can be tested in practice and which correspond – in part – to his own experience of 'second self'. He shies away, however, from the concept of a system with its implication of discipline and control and concludes the essay with a mischievous and profound thought. '… when Ouspensky had written his book, *In Search of the Miraculous,* he gave it for a subtitle *Fragments of an Unknown Teaching.* Fragments, not Unity.' (p. 146)

While this collection of essays cannot give a complete idea of Gunn's spiritual and literary journey through life, they reflect clearly the main stages of that journey and the subjects about which Gunn felt deeply. He started from the strong foundation of a powerful landscape of mountain, moor and cliff that lent itself to the evocation of wonder and metaphysical thought, and from a small subtly structured Gaelic community that inspired by its warmth of feeling and goodness. He knew that the community of his youth would disappear under the forces of economic and social change but hoped that the values that it enshrined could be preserved, perhaps in a different form , in the new order. He saw the community spirit being more likely to survive in small groups of people, and in his essays on nationalism, the small nation state being a guarantor of man's individual freedom. But it was the smallest entity of all, the human psyche, that was to be the essential ingredient in his movement towards 'the Light'. In later life his encounter with the Far Eastern philosophy of Zen thrilled him because many of the aspects of this philosophy or Way had been experienced by him in moments of revelation in his own life – often inspired by the landscape and its flora and fauna. In the essays in this collection concerned with Zen he shows that he has had intimations of a delight and harmony that were inexpressible. His ability to concentrate, his intuitive perception, practice and analysis of what he had gleaned from Zen masters and others had all helped him, but on his journey from Landscape to Light he had at all times been strictly on his own.

Notes

1 An earlier collection of essays entitled *Landscape and Light*, edited by Alistair McCleery, was published by Aberdeen University Press in 1987. This earlier collection contained a number of additional essays particularly on politics and literature.

2 See Alistair McCleery, 'The Early Novels of Neil M. Gunn', *The Bibliotheck* 10/4 (1981) pp.127-38.

3 Gunn to Ian MacArthur, 8 July 1969, Gunn Papers, Deposit 209, National Library of Scotland.

4 'The Wonder Story of the Moray Firth', written in 1968, was based on a radio talk produced by Ian Grimble and broadcast on the Scottish Home Service in April 1959.

5 J. B. Pick, *Neil M. Gunn* (Tavistock: Northcote House, 2004) p.65.

6 Gunn to Geoffrey Faber, 22 October 1950, *in* Neil M Gunn, *Selected Letters* ed. J.B. Pick (Edinburgh: Polygon, 1987) p.107

7 His feeling that his work was seen as less relevant was heightened by the fact that 'Eight Times Up' was published with a key paragraph on Samuel Beckett's *Waiting for Godot* excised by the Editor – see F. R. Hart & J. B. Pick, *Neil M. Gunn, A Highland Life* (London: John Murray, 1981) p.254.

8 By the time the last essay, 'Highland Space', was published Alexander Reid had left the editorship of the *Saltire Review*.

9 F. R. Hart, 'Neil Gunn's Drama of the Light' in ed. Cairns Craig, *The History of Scottish Literature Vol 4: Twentieth Century* (Aberdeen: Aberdeen University Press, 1987) p.99

Sources and Further Reading

Sources

Caithness & Sutherland, Wishart Books Ltd, 1935, pp. 59–76

East to Buchan, *The Scots Magazine*, Dundee, September 1939, Vol. 31, No. 6, pp. 419–424

My Bit of Britain, *The Field*, London, 2nd August, 1941, Vol. 178, No. 4623, pp. 136–137

One Fisher Went Sailing, *The Scots Magazine*, Dundee, September, 1937, Vol. 27, No. 6, pp. 414–418

The Wonder Story of the Moray Firth, *Anarchy* 86, London, April 1968, Vol. 8, No. 4, pp. 122–125

French Smack, *The Scots Magazine*, Dundee, August 1940, Vol. 33, No. 5, pp. 366–370

The First Salmon, *The Scots Magazine*, Dundee, April, 1938, Vol. 29, No. 1, pp. 17–20

Black Cattle in Lochaber, *The Scots Magazine*, Dundee, September, 1942, Vol. 37, No. 6, pp. 450–454

On Backgrounds, *The Scots Magazine*, Dundee, March, 1941, Vol. 34, No. 6, pp. 437–440

On Tradition, *The Scots Magazine*, Dundee, November, 1940, Vol. 34, No. 2, pp. 131–134

On Belief, *The Scots Magazine*, Dundee, October, 1940, Vol. 34, No. 1, pp. 51–55

On Looking at Things, *The Scots Magazine*, Dundee, June, 1940, Vol. 33, No. 3, pp. 170–174

On Magic, *The Scots Magazine*, Dundee, September, 1940, Vol. 33, No. 6, pp. 433–436

On Destruction, *The Scots Magazine*, Dundee, July, 1941, Vol. 35, No. 4, pp. 290–294

New Community of Iona, *The Scots Magazine*, Dundee, December, 1938, Vol. 30, No. 3, pp. 169–174

Landscape Inside, *Saltire Review*, Edinburgh, Autumn, 1959, Vol. 6, No. 19, pp. 43–46

Highland Space, *Saltire Review*, Edinburgh, Winter, 1961, Vol. 6, No. 23, pp. 45–48

The Heron's Legs, *Saltire Review*, Edinburgh, Summer, 1958, Vol. 5, No. 15, pp. 19–22

The Flash, *Saltire Review*, Edinburgh, Autumn, 1958, Vol. 5, No. 16, pp. 18–23

Eight Times Up, *Saltire Review*, Edinburgh, Winter, 1958, Vol. 5, No. 17, pp. 19–23

Remember Yourself, *Saltire Review*, Edinburgh, Spring, 1959, Vol. 6, No. 18, pp. 22–28
Light, *Point*, Leicester, Summer, 1968, No. 3, pp. 4–12
The Miraculous, *Point*, Leicester, Winter , 1968–69, No. 4, pp. 19–27

Further Reading
The Grey Coast, London: Jonathan Cape, 1926
Hidden Doors (Short stories), Edinburgh: The Porpoise Press, 1929
Morning Tide, Edinburgh: The Porpoise Press, 1931
The Lost Glen, Edinburgh: The Porpoise Press, 1932
Sun Circle, Edinburgh: The Porpoise Press, 1933
Butcher's Broom, Edinburgh: The Porpoise Press, 1934
Whisky & Scotland: A Practical and Spiritual Survey (History), London: George Routledge & Sons, 1935
Highland River, Edinburgh: The Porpoise Press, 1937
Off in a Boat (Travel), Edinburgh: The Porpoise Press, 1938
Wild Geese Overhead, London: Faber & Faber, 1939
Second Sight, London: Faber & Faber, 1940
The Silver Darlings, London: Faber & Faber, 1941
Young Art and Old Hector, London: Faber & Faber, 1942
Storm and Precipice and Other Pieces (Selected extracts), London: Faber & Faber, 1942
The Serpent, London: Faber & Faber, 1943
The Green Isle of the Great Deep, London: Faber & Faber, 1944
The Key of the Chest, London: Faber & Faber, 1945
The Drinking Well, London: Faber & Faber, 1946
The Shadow, London: Faber & Faber, 1948
The Silver Bough, London: Faber & Faber, 1948
The Lost Chart, London: Faber & Faber, 1949
Highland Pack (Essays), London: Faber & Faber, 1949
The White Hour, and Other Stories (Short stories), London: Faber & Faber, 1950
The Well at the World's End, London: Faber & Faber, 1951
Bloodhunt, London: Faber & Faber, 1952
The Other Landscape, London: Faber & Faber, 1954
The Atom of Delight (Autobiographical), London: Faber & Faber, 1956

Posthumous publications
Landscape and Light, Essays by Neil M. Gunn edited by Alistair McCleery, Aberdeen: Aberdeen University Press, 1987
Neil M. Gunn: Selected Letters edited by J. B. Pick, Edinburgh: Polygon, 1987
The Man Who Came Back, Short Stories and Essays edited by Margery McCulloch, Edinburgh: Polygon, 1991
Poems and related early work collected by C. J. L. Stokoe, Ampthill: Peglet Press, 1994
The Poaching at Grianan, Edinburgh: Merchiston Publishing, 2005

Major secondary literature
Burns, John, *A Celebration of the Light, Zen in the Novels of Neil Gunn*, Edinburgh: Canongate, 1988. Late in his life Neil M. Gunn came across Zen Buddhism and discovered simi-

larities and parallels to his own writing on insight and illumination. John Burns looks at this relationship and highlights the universal themes contained in Gunn's writings.

Gifford, Douglas, *Neil M. Gunn and Lewis Grassic Gibbon*, Edinburgh: Oliver & Boyd, 1983. A study comparing and contrasting these two major Scottish novelists with a detailed look at Gunn's *The Silver Darlings* and Gibbon's *A Scots Quair*.

Gunn, Dairmid and Isobel Murray (Editors), *Neil Gunn's Country, Essays in Celebration of Neil Gunn*, Edinburgh: Chambers, 1991. Range of essays by people who knew Neil Gunn the man covering both his work and his life. Contains biographical and literary assessment.

Hart, F. R. and J. B. Pick, *Neil M. Gunn: A Highland Life* by London: John Murray, 1981. The first full, and now, definitive biography of Neil Gunn by two writers who knew him well and write with insight and understanding.

Laplace, Philippe, *Les Hautes-Terres, L'Histoire et La Memoire dans les romans de Neil M Gunn*. Presses Universitaires de Franche-Compte, 2006. An analysis of history, memory and national identity derived from the novels *Sun Circle, Butcher's Broom* and *The Silver Darlings*.

McCulloch, Margery, *The Novels of Neil M. Gunn, A Critical Study*, Edinburgh: Scottish Academic Press, 1987. A critical study of all Gunn's novels which favours the earlier work and attempts to place the novels in their literary context. Explores the relationship between the fiction and non–fiction writing of Neil Gunn.

Morrison, David (Editor), *Essays on Neil M. Gunn* edited by David Morrison, Thurso: John Humphries, 1971. Contains four essays on Neil Gunn's novels including work by J. B. Caird and F. R. Hart.

Pick, J. B., *Neil M. Gunn*, Tavistock: Northcote House Publishers, 2004. An excellent succint study of Gunn's life and work by a writer who knew and corresponded with Gunn over a number of years and who writes with perception and insight.

Price, Richard, *The Fabulous Matter of Fact, The Poetics of Neil M. Gunn*, Edinburgh: Edinburgh University Press, 1991. A comprehensive look at both Gunn's written work and the background and context of his writing from the literary renaissance of the early twentieth century and its influences to its place in European modernism.

Scott, Alexander and Douglas Gifford (Editors), *Neil M. Gunn, The Man and the Writer* Edinburgh: William Blackwood, 1973. The first major work devoted to the writing of Neil Gunn. Twenty essays by major writers and critics on subjects from biography to specific novels, styles and bibliography.

Stokoe, C. J. L., *A Bibliography of the Works of Neil M. Gunn*, Aberdeen: Aberdeen University Press, 1987. A detailed and comprehensive bibliography of all Neil Gunn's writings including broadcasts and unpublished material.

Neil M. Gunn website

www.neilgunn.org.uk Contains biographical and bibliographical information, news and resources.